American English Dialects in Literature

by

EVA M. BURKETT

The Scarecrow Press, Inc.
Metuchen, N.J. & London
1978

Library of Congress Cataloging in Publication Data

Burkett, Eva Mae.
   American English dialects in literature.

   Includes index.
   1. English language in the United States--Biblio-
graphy. 2. English language--Dialects--United States
--Bibliography. 3. American literature--History
and criticism--Bibliography. 4. Regionalism in litera-
ture--Bibliography. I. Title.
Z1234.D5B87 [PE2841] 016.428'00973   78-17742
ISBN 0-8108-1151-0

To
the Memory of
My Father and Mother

CONTENTS

"A nation which is proud of its diverse heritage and of its cultural and racial variety ought to preserve its heritage of dialects."

"The Student's Right to His Own Language,"
Executive Committee of the Conference on College Composition and Communication, Boston, March 22, 1972.

PREFACE

The purpose of this book on American English dialects in literature is to give students of American literature, language, sociology, and history the opportunity to understand and to realize the effectiveness of dialect as a literary language and to determine the relationship of the American English language to American history and culture.

For several years, the chief interest of scholars of the American language has been in determining, locating, mapping out, and recording dialectal differences--regional, local, and social. This book provides information and material for comparing the language data acquired by these scholars with the language used by literary artists, who in the main depend on their own long association and experience with local people for their knowledge of the language they use as a medium for presenting character, identifying periods and locales, and creating mood or tone. Many writers create their own systems of presenting the language, particularly in their use of respelling to indicate pronunciation, so that reading of dialectal writing may be difficult for those not familiar with the particular dialect used.

The idea that the use of dialect in literature belongs to our early history and is largely the province of local color writers and humorists is disproved by the extent to which it is used by writers of the twentieth century. Although modern methods of communication and opportunities for education have done much to blur or erase the broader elements of dialectal variations, there are still sufficient recognizable differences in vocabulary, in pronunciation, and in grammatical forms to make the study of the variations in the American language both profitable and interesting. It is hoped that differences will continue to exist, for as Raven I. McDavid, Jr., says, local forms in speech "help to maintain one's individual dignity in a homogenizing world."

Students of American society, particularly anthropologists, will be interested in tracing the history of settlements, the migrations, the occupations, the interests and cultural levels as these are revealed in the language, for, in many cases, linguistic data are more dependable than the available historical data, and the differences that appear in speech also appear in other cultural phenomena. They will see that dialect differences are a result of differences in experience and are not indications of intellectual, physical, or moral differences. "Language is the medium through which the cultural relationships of a people are expressed and ... without the knowledge of linguistic principles by which an understanding of the native language may be obtained, the anthropologist can attain only the most superficial description of a culture."[1]

Students of foreign languages, and especially those interested in teaching English as a foreign language, will find the section on the language of immigrants valuable as illustrations of some of the difficulties encountered by those learning English as a second language. Students of fields other than English will find the basic linguistic information provided by linguistic scholars an interesting addition to their cultural knowledge. Accounts of the dialects of particular groups give helpful information concerning causes and results. F. O. Matthiessen says that "an artist's use of language is the most sensitive index to cultural history, since a man can articulate only what he is, and what he has been made by the society of which he is a willing or unwilling part."[2]

The lists of writers and their works that provide examples of various forms of American English dialects are only representative and may be easily expanded by students who wish to examine further the use and literary effectiveness of colloquial speech.

The section on "Analysis of Dialect in Literature" shows how critics examine the use of dialect as a literary medium. The paper in the Appendix, written by a beginning freshman college student, is included to show how inexperienced language students may approach the analysis of literary dialect by first examining the writing for characteristics of the dialect, making notes of the examples found, and using these lists as the basis of conclusions about the writer's use of dialect. The outline includes the basic linguistic items: pronunciation, words and expressions, and grammatical forms.

"Language is the soil of thought, and our own especially is a rich leaf-mould, the slow deposit of ages, the
shed foliage of feeling, fancy, and imagination, which has
suffered an earth-change, that the vocal forest, as Howells
called it, may clothe itself anew with living green.   There
is death in the dictionary; and where language is too strictly
limited by convention, the ground for expression to grow in
is limited also; and we get a potted literature, Chinese
dwarfs instead of healthy trees."

> --James Russell Lowell, "Introduction," Biglow Pa-
> pers, Second Series, 1866, in The Complete Writ-
> ings of James Russell Lowell.   New York: AMS
> Press, Inc., 1966, XI, 11.

CHAPTER I

AMERICAN ENGLISH DIALECTS

Introduction

     Although any native speaker of American English will
be understood by members of any American community,
there exist differences in vocabulary, in pronunciation, and
in grammatical forms and sentence patterns sufficiently evident to enable students of language to identify particular sections as dialectal areas.   For many years, it was customary
to label three main dialect areas of American English--the
New England, the Southern, and General American--but data
gathered by field workers for the Linguistic Atlas of the
United States and Canada and by individual students have enabled linguistic scholars to draw lines of dialect areas with
more accuracy.

     Albert C. Baugh suggests that it now seems best to
recognize seven regional dialect areas: Eastern New England, New York City, Middle Atlantic, Western Pennsylvania,
Southern Mountain, Southern, and General American. [3]   Albert Marckwardt, basing his concepts on the materials presented in Hans Kurath's A Word Geography of the Eastern
United States, 1949, and other more recent studies, accepts
the three general divisions but points out that each area
must be further divided into more specific sub-dialect areas,
each having its own characteristic forms. [4]   Hans Kurath
labels the three major dialect areas along the Atlantic Coast
as the North, the Midland, and the South, and further divides them into eighteen minor speech areas. [5]   George L.
Trager says that the English spoken in the United States can
be divided into eight areas with subdivisions in each area. [6]

     Earlier (1947), C. K. Thomas, basing his conclusions
on an analysis of recordings of the speech of native Americans, designated seven major regional dialect areas in his

1

Phonetics of American English. In a later edition (1958) of the same book, he increased the number of areas to ten: Eastern New England, New York City, Middle Atlantic, Southern, Western Pennsylvania, Southern Mountain, Central Midland, Southwest, North Central, and Northwest.[7] Kurath uses vocabulary as the basis of division. Thomas uses pronunciation as his evidence. Arthur J. Bronstein says that conclusions about regional pronunciations are still tentative and must wait upon the interpretations and analyses of field data already collected or to be collected. He says, however, that the following conclusions may be made from the evidence already in:

> (1) A clearly defined Midland speech separates the regional dialects of the North and South in the eastern part of the United States. (2) The political boundaries of the North and South have proved inaccurate for designating speech areas. (3) The older designations, 'New England Speech,' or 'Eastern Speech,' are misleading. Coastal New England, western New England, New York City, and the Hudson Valley are fairly distinct speech areas and are better thought of separately or grouped as subareas of the northeastern part of the United States.[8]

For this study, the limitations of the dialect areas will not be definite since there is still not complete agreement as to the major dialect areas, but the study will follow in general the boundaries of the three main areas along the Atlantic Coast with their boundaries extended as people moved westward. Various sub-groups will be included wherever warranted. Thus Negro speech, not a regional division but certainly important in literature, will be shown as it is used by both Negro and White writers, with attention given to special dialects such as Gullah. Since the study is concerned with the use of dialects in literature rather than with the analysis of linguistic data acquired from contemporary users, the chief interest is in the examination of the dialect to determine its adaptability and effectiveness for literary purposes: for presenting character, for identifying periods and locales, for creating mood or tone. The dialect used by writers may not be exactly the same as that described by linguistic scholars for the same area since the writer uses the language with which he is familiar as a part of his native background or as the result of long association with native speakers of the dialect, and he adapts it to suit his purposes. The writer may have a poor ear or he may not know how to represent exactly the speech he hears. Thus his dialect is faulty. There are also elements of the spoken language that cannot be represented in writing--stress, pitch, nasality, drawl, voice quality, speech tune--except as these are explained by the writer.

It is not expected that writers of the same dialect will use the same forms. "Since a dialect is merely the sum of the particulars which a given observer synthesizes into an impression of a homogeneous speech," says George Philip Krapp, "it may well happen that two different persons observing the speech of the same group will base their impressions of unity upon widely differing details. One person will regard one feature of speech as quintessentially the mark of a certain dialect and another will choose a different feature or set of features."[9]

For assessing the accuracy of the literary dialect, available scholarly knowledge will serve as the standard. All minor dialect areas are not represented in the selections since literary qualities as well as availability have been determining factors in the choice of selections.

Definition of Dialect

But what is dialect? To some people dialect means the speech of the uneducated, or the speech of a person from another section whose pronunciation and word choice differ from their own, or the speech of someone who is speaking a language not his native one. G. L. Brook says that he regards dialect as any subdivision of a language that can be associated with a particular group of speakers smaller than the group which shares the common language. Thus British and American English are major dialects of the language known as English, but each can be further subdivided into a number of sub-dialects. He suggests, also, that the basis of subdivision of a language into dialects need not be geographical, for it may be social or occupational.[10] Edward Sapir says, "A group of dialects is merely the socialized form of the universal tendency to individual variation in speech. These variations affect the phonetic form of the language, its formal characteristics, its vocabulary and such prosodic features as intonation and stress. No known language, unless it be artifically preserved for liturgical or other nonpopular uses, has ever been known to resist the tendency to split up into dialects, any one of which may in the long run assume the status of an independent language."[11]

Raven I. McDavid, Jr., offers this definition:

> ... It is simply a habitual variety of a language,
> regional or social. It is set off from all other
> such habitual varieties by a unique combination of
> language features: words and meanings, grammat-
> ical forms, phrase structures, pronunciations, pat-
> terns of stress and intonation. No dialect is simply
> good or bad in itself; its prestige comes from the
> prestige of those who use it. But every dialect is
> in itself a legitimate form of the language, a valid
> instrument of human communication, and something
> worthy of serious study. [12]

McDavid also points out that a dialect is not something
archaic and strange; it is not confined to the speech of older
people in rural areas; and it is not restricted to "sloppy, ir-
responsible usage." It may even, as in the writings of William Faulkner, "be transmuted into the idiom of the greatest
literature." Dialect is a term to indicate that the speech of
one group is different in some ways from that of another
group, and it may refer to the speech of the educated. "It
may be essentially the speech of the uneducated, as Cockney
is the speech of the uneducated Londoner. It may be regional, as the speech of West Riding farmers differs from that
of Devonshire farmers. And particularly in the United States,
it may have both regional and social dimensions; educated
American speech has many regional varieties--south Texas,
Boston, the Hudson Valley, Iowa, Vermont--but in any region, say the Boston area, the speech of the natives will
have some common characteristics regardless of social level,
though in each region educated speech will differ from the uneducated. "[13]

Thus dialects are divided basically in two ways: by
regions and by social groups. However, George L. Trager
divides dialects into five groups: geographical, social, standard, literary, and colonial. [14] G. L. Brook says that class
dialect is of the most interest to the novelist and the dramatist, and he points out that the preoccupation of the Victorians
with class distinctions is demonstrated in the many references
to speech as a measure of social standing that are to be found
in Victorian novels. [15]

Social dialects reflect differences in the social order.
The dialect spoken by educated people and by people in au-
thority becomes the prestige dialect which is thus the dialect

to be imitated by those seeking to acquire social status.
Members of the social class who speak the prestige dialect
often feel more free and less bound by the dialect and may
thus tend to depart from their dialect whenever they please.
It should also be noted that there may be sharp differences
in the speech of those who speak the prestige dialects. But
within its own area each may be acceptable. Sumner Ives
says that he observed some phonological characteristics which
occur consistently in the speech of Negroes whose social status is the lowest. During the course of an interview "some
striking correlations between voice qualifier--especially
whine--and the subject matter are evident. The dialectal
significance of this lies in the fact that the social status of
the informant affects the relationship between voice qualifier
and subject matter."[16] McDavid says that no one has yet
worked out a comparison of the way dialects differ in stress
and pitch and transitions between syllables. "Yet these differences are felt so intuitively in the South that by them one
can often place an inhabitant of the Coastal Plain within a
few miles of his home--even if, as with some clergymen and
other public performers, he has taken pains to conceal his
origins."[17] There has also been no systematic study of regional grammatical differences in written American English.[18]

Regional Dialects

Although social dialects may take different directions
in different localities, American regional dialects are largely the results of the same forces. They have their origin
in the speech of the people who settled the separate colonies.
Thus the major dialects of the eastern coast reflect the
British dialects of the early settlers. As the people moved
westward, they carried their language with them, changing
it as they mingled with new immigrants from other countries
or as the new environment demanded change--in the new use
of old locutions or in the creation of new ones.

Raven I. McDavid, Jr., says that since there are no
"pure dialects," dialect differences may be explained by a
combination of forces. These may be summarized as follows: (1) Any large or influential element in the early population of an area can be expected to contribute materially
to the speech of that area. (2) Migrations carry dialects
along their routes. (3) Old political and ecclesiastical boundaries may have brought about dialect divisions. (4) Physical
geography is important. Passes in mountain ranges may de-

termine the routes of migrations. (5) A cultural center will
exert an influence on less important communities. (6) The
dialect of an area may reflect its social structure. (7) Dialect may reflect the presence of new immigrants with different linguistic and cultural backgrounds. [19] In order, then,
to understand American dialects as they are at present, one
must know the history of the people who speak these dialects.

Settlements of the Colonies and the Movement Westward

The settlers who came to New England and Virginia
in the seventeenth century were mainly from the southeastern and southern counties of England, although the south
Midlands and the west were more fully represented in Virginia than in New England. The Quakers who settled along
the Delaware and the settlers in eastern Pennsylvania came
from the northern part of England. The Scotch-Irish who
settled in Pennsylvania also spoke Northern English. Thus
the colonists who began the settlement of America spoke the
language of the places from which they migrated.

The westward movement from the eastern coastal regions in the eighteenth century was mainly in three large
settlement waves. The first began in the western section of
New England, west of the Connecticut River line, and traveled across New York and northern Pennsylvania to the Great
Lakes. In the second, Pennsylvanians moved south through
western Maryland to the Carolinas and Georgia. Later their
descendants crossed the mountains into Kentucky, Tennessee,
Ohio, Indiana, and Illinois. Others moved into what is now
West Virginia. In the third large migration, Southern settlers moved across the Gulf States into eastern Texas. [20]

According to Charlton Laird, the back country people
moved into Kentucky and Tennessee, into the southern portion of the states north of the Ohio River and south to the
Gulf of Mexico, up the Arkansas River into Arkansas, into
Colorado, and south again to Texas after the War with Mexico. [21] He says that the movements of these people can be
traced by the speakers they left behind them: those "who
fished with red worms, had fireboards, and used tow sacks,
croker sacks, and pokes. " The people in the lowlands
moved west only after the flat lands filled up and the Choctaw
and Cherokee Indians were moved out, but they finally moved
into Texas, "fishing with earthworms, fishworms, or fish
bait as they went, putting their produce into guano sacks and

gunny sacks, and building houses having mantels and mantel boards."

Louis A. Muinzer attributes the uniformity of American English as well as its raciness and vitality to the mobility of the American people, a mobility that is personal, social, and linguistic. He says that from "the viewpoint of dialect, there are four major types of movement in American English: (1) the conquest of folk-dialects of the Atlantic coast by regional forms; (2) the spread of the regional dialects inland from the east; (3) the mass movement of the educated citizenry from substandard social dialect forms to the national good-usage written and regional varieties of good-usage spoken English; and (4) the easy movement of neologisms, slangy or otherwise, through the regional and social dialects."[22]

Raven I. McDavid, Jr., thinks that differences in the way educated Americans use their language have been created by several factors: from colonial times, local and regional loyalties have been stronger than national ones; the constituents of the dialect mixture were different in every community; slave labor in the South interfered with new colonies of foreign-language groups; the stratified society in the South created greater differences between the educated and uneducated speech but contributed to a more informal style of speaking.[23]

Dialect in Literature

Why do writers use dialect? One of the main reasons is to add vigor and freshness to their writings. As James Russell Lowell points out, "There is death in the dictionary; and, where living language is too strictly limited by convention, the ground for expression to grow in is limited also; and we get a potted literature, Chinese dwarfs instead of healthy trees.... The first postulate of an original literature is that a people should use their language instinctively and unconsciously, as if it were a lively part of their growth and personality, not as the mere torpid book of education or inheritance."[24] George Steiner even suggests that "it may well be that culture and societies die when their uses of language atrophy."[25]

Dialect may be used to identify a character by showing his educational and cultural background as well as his

general attitudes, and it may reflect the characteristics of
the people using it. Grammatical forms and usage are apt
to reflect social differences; word choice and pronunciation
tend to reflect regional differences. Carson McCullers in
The Heart Is a Lonely Hunter has Doctor Benedict Mady Cope-
land, a Negro medical doctor, use precise standard speech,
even with his own children who speak the dialect of the uneducated Southerner in a small town in Georgia, to symbolize
his refusal to bend to the injustices he and the other members
of his race suffer. Here the contrast in language carries the
idea. A character's mental acuteness and his poetic imagination, or the lack of these qualities, may be revealed through
his inventiveness in language or through his limited vocabulary or his habitual use of worn-out or static expressions.
A study of the figurative language of John Steinbeck's Okies
or of Marjorie Kinnan Rawlings's Florida Crackers shows
their inventiveness and their poetic imagination, factors that
have little to do with formal education.

Dialect may be used for comic effect, but that is not
always its chief purpose and its use may have the opposite
effect. Dialect must be used sparingly and with care to its
communicability, although entire novels have been written in
dialect. Unless the reader is familiar with the dialect or
has knowledge of people who speak the dialect, his understanding and appreciation of the writing will be lessened.
The writer tries to create an illusion that a certain kind of
character is speaking. To avoid difficulty for the reader,
many writers do not try to reproduce dialect exactly or to
continue its use throughout a composition after it has been
sufficiently suggested, and Faulkner does in "Barn Burning."
"Dialect is like garlic," says Thames Williamson. "A little
of it is sometimes fine, too much of it is horrible."[26] "The
purpose of literary dialect," says George Philip Krapp, "is
not so much to arouse wonder as to secure sympathetic attention."[27]

The use of dialect in literature is not new. It was
used by Chaucer and by Shakespeare and by many other writers who know how to make language serve their literary needs.
As Leo Rosten points out, the proper use of dialect is creative, not literal, "for the writer transforms that which he
hears into that which you could not. There is a magic in
dialect which can liberate us from the prison of the familiar." Earlier in the same article, Rosten says, "... Dialect must seduce the eye to reach the ear and be orchestrated in the brain. It must tantalize without irritating, and

defer without frustrating. It must carry a visual promise to the reader that what he does not instantly recognize can be deciphered with ease and will be rewarded with pleasure. The reader must be cued into making what he thinks is his own special and private discovery--a discovery of delight which, he suspects, neither the character nor the author fully appreciates. "[28]

Joel Chandler Harris agrees with Rosten. In referring to his own use of dialect he says: "... If the language of Uncle Remus fails to give vivid hints of the really poetic imagination of the Negro; if it fails to embody the quaint and homely humor which was his most prominent characteristic; if it does not suggest a certain picturesque sensitiveness--a curious exaltation of mind and temperament not to be defined by words--then I have reproduced the form of the dialect merely, and not the essence, and my attempt may be accounted a failure. "[29]

Sumner Ives says that the literary dialect of a reliable author may "supply details, especially in vocabulary and structure, that are missing from the phonetician's record. There is possible service also to the historical study of English.... The evidence given in a carefully and competently written literary dialect regarding pronunciations is similar in many respects to the evidence on which some historical conclusions are based. "[30] Folk usages are usually not corruptions of standard English but traditional forms kept long after they have been discarded by standard users. The skillful use of dialect in writing contributes to literary excellence. The representation of the life of a people in their dialect is a form of history.

Studies in American English Dialects (General)

1. Allen, Harold B. The Linguistic Atlas of the Upper Midwest. Three volumes. Volume I. University of Minnesota Press, 1973. 425 pp. In two parts. Part A, The Upper Midwest Project; Part B, The Lexicon. Volume II. University of Minnesota Press, 1975. 92 pp. The Grammar. Volume III. University of Minnesota Press, 1976. 362 pp. The Pronunciation.
A study of regional and social variations in English spoken by native speakers of the language in Minnesota, Iowa, North Dakota, South Dakota, and Nebraska. Based on field interviews with 208 local residents representing three generations and three socio-educational groups.

2. Allen, Harold B. "The Primary Dialect Areas of the Upper Midwest," in Readings in Applied Linguistics. Edited by Harold B. Allen. New York: Appleton-Century-Crofts, 2nd edition, 1954, pp. 231-241.

Allen uses the material provided by the Linguistic Atlas of the North Central States and material provided by field-work for the Linguistic Atlas of the Upper Midwest to determine the Midland-Northern relationship in the region immediately west of the North Central states. He concludes: the primary Midland-Northern dialect contrast of the Atlantic coast states is maintained in the Upper Midwest; the distinction is particularly clear between the lower two-thirds and the upper third of Iowa; the distinction is less clear west of the Missouri river; in general, Northern speech seems to be yielding to Midland; one Northern enclave occurs in Midland territory and a probable enclave occurs in Northern territory.

3. Atwood, E. Bagby. "The Methods of American Dialectology," Zeitschrift für Mundartforschung, XXX, No. 1 (1963), 1-29. Reprinted in Readings in American Dialectology. Edited by Harold B. Allen and Gary N. Underwood. New York: Appleton-Century-Crofts, 1971, pp. 5-35. In English.

A scholarly discussion of the methods used in studying American dialects. The discussion is organized in three parts: the work of American lexicographers and of the American Dialect Society and its publications; the contributions of linguistic geographers in preparing the Linguistic Atlas of New England, A Word Geography of the Eastern United States, A Survey of Verb Forms in the Eastern United States; and extensions of the Atlas work in such studies as Principal and Subsidiary Dialect Areas in the North Central States, Grammatical Differences in the North Central States, The Regional Vocabulary of Texas.

4. Atwood, E. Bagby. The Regional Vocabulary of Texas. Austin: The University of Texas Press, 1962. 273 pp. 125 word maps.

A vocabulary study concerned primarily with Texas. The material was collected through interviews which used a questionnaire pertaining strictly to vocabulary and based on the work sheets of the Linguistic Atlas, with additions aimed at eliciting words belonging particularly to the region. A number of senior and graduate students at the University of Texas served as interviewers, and colleagues from area colleges and universities used the questionnaire with their students.

5. Atwood, E. Bagby. A Survey of Verb Forms in the Eastern United States. Ann Arbor: University of Michigan Press, 1953. 43 pp. 31 figures.

A study of the verb forms in the Eastern United States based on the Linguistic Atlas field records of over 1400 informants. Of these records, 413 were gathered in New England, about 475 in the Middle Atlantic states, and about 550 in the South Atlantic states. An analysis was made of the tense forms, the personal forms of the present indicative, number and agreement, negative forms, the infinitive and present participle, and phrases.

6. Baugh, Albert C. "The American Dialects," in A History of the English Language. New York: Appleton-Century-Crofts, Second edition, 1957, pp. 436-446.

A general survey of studies concerned with American dialects with full references in footnotes. Baugh accepts the explanation that the various American dialects are a product of the language spoken by the original settlers, especially in the New England area. He recognizes seven regional dialects in the United States, but suggests that education and the absence of social classes tend to eliminate language differences. Baugh is particularly concerned with distinctive features of pronunciation.

7. Contemporary English, Change and Variation. Introductions by Irwin Feigenbaum, Philip B. Gove, Roger W. Shuy. Edited by David L. Shores. Philadelphia: J. B. Lippincott Company, 1972. 380 pp. (Paper)

A book designed to provide college students and teachers on all levels with information about language that will "serve to awaken the reader's curiosity about language variation, to deepen his knowledge about standard and nonstandard English, and to establish informed and accurate attitudes and approaches toward language in human affairs." The essays by important linguists are grouped into three sections: "Standard and Nonstandard English: Temporal, Regional, and Social Variations," with introduction by Roger W. Shuy; "Standard English: The Problem of Definition," with introduction by Philip B. Gove; and "Standard and Nonstandard English: Learning and Teaching Problems," with introduction by Irwin Feigenbaum. Full notes are given, pp. 347-363. A selected bibliography is included.

8. Davis, Lawrence M. "Social Dialectology in America: A Critical Survey," Journal of English Linguistics, IV (March, 1970), 46-56.

A discussion of the work of The Linguistic Atlas of the United States and Canada and the use of its data in other studies, of the contributions of C. C. Fries in his American English Grammar, of the attacks made on the work of the Atlas and the effect of these attacks on the schools and on the attitudes toward the use of the data-based conclusions of the dialectologists. Other attacks on the sampling methods of the dialectologists were made by William Labov in The Social Stratification of English in New York City and by Lee A. Pederson in The Pronunciation of English in Metropolitan Chicago. The use of the field worker's impressions to determine the social class of informants was also questioned. In their study of Detroit speech, Roger Shuy and his associates used Labov's methods, and Walter Wolfram, using the records of forty-eight informants for Shuy's original random sample, made a study of the speech of Black informants. Davis concludes that although the Atlas records have serious drawbacks, they are still useful and remain relatively "unplumbed."

10. Eggleston, Edward. "Mother English, Folk-Speech, Folk-Lore, and Literature," in The Transit of Civilization from England to America in the Seventeenth Century. New York: Peter Smith, 1933, pp. 96-140. Copyright 1900.
A discussion of the language brought by the English colonists to America and the language that resulted from contacts with a new environment. Eggleston mentions particularly the influence of the Indian language on the vocabulary, the pronunciation that some of the settlers brought with them that became known as the Yankee dialect, the effect of social conditions on American speech, the Gullah dialect on the coast of South Carolina, and the use of proverbs and of superstitious lore.

11. Ives, Sumner. "Use of Field Materials in the Determination of Dialect Groupings," The Quarterly Journal of Speech, XLI (December, 1955), 359-364.
A discussion of the methods used by Hans Kurath, E. Bagby Atwood, C. K. Thomas, C. M. Wise, George Trager, and Sumner Ives to collect data for determining speech boundaries in pronunciation. Kurath and those who worked with the Linguistic Atlas used isoglosses determined by the outer limits of specific instances and based on phonetic transcriptions made by selected informants for field workers. C. K. Thomas used tape recordings of prepared texts read by informants. He located boundaries where majority usage shifts. Trager was interested in the development of a pro-

cedure for representing the phonemic structure of any variety of American English. Ives worked with the Urban Life Research Institute at Tulane University to try to determine a means of defining cultural groups and for estimating social mobility. Using transcriptions of tape recordings of interviews with Negro subjects, Ives was able to isolate a number of words the pronunciation of which was socially significant. His estimate of the cultural groupings fitted into the hypothesis about class structure among New Orleans Negroes which another member of the Institute had formulated on other evidence. Ives observed a striking correlation between voice qualifier, especially whine, and the subject matter, a situation based on the social status of the informant.

12. Johnson, Falk. "How We Got Our Dialects," American Mercury, LXIV (January, 1947), 66-70.
According to Johnson, American dialects are the results of transplanted British and European dialects, of dialectal transfusions from other sources such as that of the Indians, and of local linguistic creations.

13. Krapp, George Philip. "The Psychology of Dialect Writing," The Bookman, LXII (July, 1926), 522-527.
Krapp thinks that the interest in using dialect in American literature is not a reflection of a folk movement in literature but is the invention of sophisticated literary artists who must always keep their eyes on the effect and must select or reject material as it suits or does not suit their purposes. He says that dialect literature is not a popular literature but is in reality a highbrow literature, "the work of persons who stand superiorly aloof from popular life and picture it amusedly, patronizingly, photographically, satirically, sentimentally, as their tastes incline them." Krapp discusses particularly Yiddish and Negro English, which he says are disappearing as speech but are more suited for literary purposes, and the satirical use of dialect by Ring Lardner.

14. Kurath, Hans. "Dialect Areas, Settlement Areas, and Culture Areas in the United States," in The Cultural Approach to History. Edited by Caroline F. Ware. Port Washington, N.Y.: Kennikat Press, Inc., 1940, pp. 331-345.
Kurath summarizes the scholarly work that has been done to show the relation of the speech of the American people to the history of settlements and to the influence of trade and culture areas. The linguist has added his contribution to the work of the historian, the geographer, and the sociologist to our understanding of regional and national culture.

Kurath mentions particularly the importance of The Dictionary of American English, The Linguistic Atlas of the United
States and Canada, The Handbook of the Linguistic Geography
of New England, and the contributions of H. L. Mencken and
George Philip Krapp.

15. Kurath, Hans. Handbook of the Linguistic Geography of New England. Providence: Brown University Press,
1939. 240 pp. 2 plates. Reprinted in 1954 by the American Council of Learned Societies. Second edition, with Index
prepared by Audrey Duckert. New York: AMS Press, 1972.
    The purpose of the Handbook is to present an outline
of the regional and social dialects of New England and to provide the apparatus for the critical evaluation and historical
interpretation of the materials contained in the Linguistic Atlas of New England. In Chapter I the two major dialect areas of New England are described. Chapter II provides a description of the field work and the editorial procedure as well
as a bibliography of studies in linguistic geography. Chapter
III, written by Marcus L. Hansen and including a bibliography
of New England regional and local history, gives a history of
the New England population as a background for the historical
interpretation of New England speech. Chapters IV and V include a discussion of the phonetic alphabet and the work sheets.
Chapter VI gives a description of the communities and of the
informants.

16. Kurath, Hans, and Raven I. McDavid, Jr. The
Pronunciation of English in the Atlantic States. Based upon
the collections of the Linguistic Atlas of the Eastern United
States. Ann Arbor: University of Michigan Press, 1961.
182 pp. 180 maps.
    The first four chapters are the work chiefly of Kurath;
the fifth chapter is the work of McDavid. The first chapter
concerns the character of the source material, the design of
the questionnaire, the approach to an analysis of the vowel
system, and the extent to which features of pronunciation are
systematized. Chapter 2 discusses the regional dialects of
cultivated speech, based upon the usage of 157 speakers. Regional and social differences in the pronunciation of vowel
phonemes are presented in Chapter 3. Chapter 4 treats
of consonant /r/ and the pronunciation of certain vowels.
Chapter 5 deals with the regionally and socially varying
incidence of vowel and consonant phonemes in the vocabulary.

17. Kurath, Hans. A Word Geography of the East-ern United States. Ann Arbor: University of Michigan Press, 1949. 88 pp. 163 figures of word boundaries.

Concerned with the regional and local vocabulary of the Eastern United States and based largely on materials collected for the Linguistic Atlas of New England and by the interviews of Guy S. Lowman, this study covers the areas included in all of the original thirteen states and the areas settled after the Revolution before 1800 except Kentucky. The book contains three chapters and a glossary of seven pages. Chapter I provides a perspective of the settlements and speech areas, the national stocks and social classes, the levels of speech, ranges of the vocabulary, and the European sources with American innovations. Chapter II discusses the three main speech areas: Northern, Midland, and Southern and their combinations. Chapter III shows regional and local words in topical arrangement. Kurath says that one fact seems to be fully established by the study: "There is an extensive Midland speech area that lies between the traditionally 'Northern' and 'Southern' areas" that corresponds to the Pennsylvania settlement area. He also says that to speak of a linguistic Mason and Dixon Line is an erroneous inference.

18. McDavid, Raven I., Jr. "Dialects: British and American Standard and Nonstandard," in Linguistics Today. Edited by Archibald Hill. New York and London: Basic Books, Inc., 1969, pp. 79-88.

McDavid defines dialect as "any habitual variety of a language, regional or social," but, he says, all dialects are legitimate forms of the language. In any locality, the speech of some people or groups of people is considered better than that of others and thus the cause of the development of social dialects. The basic cause of regional dialects is in the nature of the original settlements, but political, commercial, and educational forces also influence dialect patterns. In the United States, it is not difficult to trace the extensions of the regional patterns of speech established by the end of the eighteenth century--Northern, Midland, and Southern; even west of the Mississippi river--although the most characteristically local forms of speech stayed at home and did not migrate. McDavid says that the complex interrelationships of historical, regional, social, and racial forces can be illustrated by a single linguistic feature: the lack of the -s form for the third-person singular present indicative.

19. McDavid, Raven I., Jr. "Dialect Geography and Social Science Problems," Social Forces, XXV (December, 1946), 168-172.

McDavid says that the command of a language is necessary for an understanding of the culture in which the language is spoken.   Without a knowledge of linguistic principles
even the anthropologist can attain only the most superficial
description of a culture.   The importance of language as a
mirror of culture can be demonstrated by dialect differences
in American English.   Pronunciation and rapidity of speech
are a reflection not of the climate but of the speech used by
those who settled in the area and of contacts of the inhabitants with speakers of the dialects.   The extent of local dia-
lect-areas provides an accurate picture of the extent of early settlements.   Trade and communication are also reflected
in the perpetuation of some words and pronunciations.   Isolation of a community may determine speech forms different
from those of neighboring communities.   Vocabulary reflects
the relationships between urban and rural life as well as the
traditional economy of a region, the change in size and or-
ganization of a family as well as the political, social, and
religious structure of the community.   Language also reveals
prejudice in one's background.   "The more one investigates
American dialects, the more impressive is the evidence that
linguistic phenomena are an essential part of the data that
must be considered in the analysis involving the social
sciences. "

20.   McDavid, Raven I. , Jr.   "Folk Speech, " in Our
Living Traditions.   Edited by Tristram Potter Coffin.   New
York: Basic Books, Inc. , 1968, pp. 228-237.
The study of folk speech involves not only the track-
ing down of Middle English or Celtic survivals in remote
areas, but the discovery of innovations and the ways in which
they were disseminated.   It is related to the general study of
the regional and social distribution of linguistic forms, and
to their relationships to the historical and social and cultural
forces.   It concerns not only the distribution of old-fashioned
words but older grammatical constructions as well as patterns
of stress.   It even includes gestures.   The recording of
quaint and curious language must be accompanied by a study
of the significance of the records.   Evidence must be gathered
with particular features of language in mind.   Then must come
the charting of the patterns of distribution and the explanations.

21.   McDavid, Raven I. , Jr.   "Sense and Nonsense
about American Dialects, " PMLA, LXXXI, No. 2 (May, 1966),
7-17.
McDavid discusses some of the nonsensical attitudes
towards dialects, gives his definition of dialect, and concludes

with nine "clear statements" about the facts of American dialects and their significance.

22. McDavid, Raven I. , Jr. "The Dialects of American English, " in W. Nelson Francis, The Structure of American English. New York: Ronald Press Company, 1958, pp. 480-543.

McDavid discusses American dialects under eight main heads: dialect differences and their causes, linguistic geography, progress of the American Linguistic Atlas, forces underlying dialect distribution in America, the principal dialect areas of the United States, the influence of foreign-language settlements, class dialects, and literary dialects.

23. McDavid, Raven I. , Jr. "Some Social Differences in Pronunciation, " Language Learning, IV (1952-1953), 102-116.

McDavid says that some pronunciations that are not accepted nationally may carry connotations of social prestige or the lack of it depending on the area in which they are found. Differences in pronunciation are not always determined by social and educational background but may be the result of geographical differences. Thus some regional speech is standard although not nationally recognized as such.

24. Marckwardt, Albert H. "Principal and Subsidiary Dialect Areas in the North-Central States, " in Readings in American Dialectology. Edited by Harold B. Allen and Gary N. Underwood. New York: Appleton-Century-Crofts, 1971, pp. 74-82. Reprinted from PADS, XXVII (1957), 3-15.

Basing his discussion on Kurath's Word Geography of the Eastern United States, Marckwardt outlines the subsidiary dialect areas and tries to account for the various linguistic boundaries and speech features. He concludes that three major population movements--the migration from New York and New England into the northern part of the territory, that from Virginia and the Carolinas into Kentucky and then into southern Ohio and Illinois and most of Indiana, and the migration from Pennsylvania--provided the dialect mixture found in these areas.

25. Marckwardt, Albert H. "Regional and Social Variations, " in American English. New York: Oxford University Press, 1958, pp. 131-150.

A discussion of the work of the Linguistic Atlas and of the studies that followed, the various dialect boundaries and the characteristic forms in vocabulary and pronunciation

of the subdialect areas. Marckwardt attributes the differences
in language to settlement history; to the industrial revolution
which concentrated people in cities resulting in changed cultural patterns, particularly where there was a concentration
of immigrants; the movement westward and environmental
factors such as topography, climate, plant and animal life;
the different types of institutions and practices which developed in various parts of the country; new inventions or development which acquire different names in different places.
Word meanings and inflectional forms, especially in substandard use, also change.

26. Marshall, Howard Wight, and John Michael Vlach.
"Toward a Folklife Approach to American Dialects," American Speech, XLVIII, No. 3-4 (Fall-Winter, 1973), 163-191.
Marshall and Vlach believe that information about material culture can help establish dialect boundaries, to identify the presence of lexical items, and to aid in clarifying the
history of speech patterns. In this paper, three dialect problems are analyzed: the interaction of dialect and artifact patterns in Pennsylvania and the Valley of Virginia; Southern and
Midland dialect interaction in the Deep South; and folklife and
dialect patterns in Southern Indiana. The Mid-Atlantic mater-
ial-cultural source area is important for presenting folk cultures since it has influence in both the North and the South.
The most important facet of folklife to have its roots in the
area is horizontal log construction. Other elements of material culture include the dulcimer, the Kentucky long rifle,
and four types of barns. Dialect items match the material
items. Since there was material interaction in both northern
and southern directions, dialect homogeneity was encouraged
in the Southern and Midland dialect areas. The authors conclude that the folklife approach to dialects is not only a tool
for explanation but is also an effective analytical method.
They suggest that the study of material culture is particularly useful in understanding dialect pockets.

27. Matthews, Brander. "The Permanent Utility of
Dialect," Yale Review, X (January, 1921), 338-348.
Matthews argues for the use of the simple and vigor-
ous words of everyday life as opposed to the use of "inkhorn
terms" and of inflated language. He discusses the ways dialects enrich language and the way a particular dialect may
become the heart of a language. "In all modern languages--
and no doubt in all ancient languages also--the standard speech
is but the ripe development of a dialect which was originally
local to a restricted area." "When a dialect is lifted from

its lowly condition and becomes a national tongue, it is like
the banyan tree of the Orient--from every far-extending
branch it sends down tendrils which suck nourishment from
the soil immediately beneath them and so serve to support
the limbs from which they had hung dependent. "

28. Mencken, H. L. "Dialects, " in The American
Language. Abridged, with annotations and new material by
Raven I. McDavid, Jr. , with the assistance of David W.
Maurer. New York: Alfred A. Knopf, 1971, pp. 448-478.
A discussion of the early studies of American dialects,
of the work of the Linguistic Atlas of the United States and
Canada, and of the dialect areas of the United States with
their characteristics, including the dialects of Hawaii. Full
footnotes provide excellent references for further study.

29. Readings in American Dialectology. Edited by
Harold B. Allen and Gary N. Underwood. New York: Appleton-Century-Crofts, 1971. 584 pp.
A collection of articles on American dialects organized into two parts: regional dialects and social dialects.
Part One contains two general articles on dialects, nine articles on area studies, eight single-feature articles, five articles presenting the comparative approach, and five articles
on dialect theory. Part Two consists of twelve articles that
show the social aspects of dialectology. A bibliography of
twenty-eight pages of articles and books on dialectology follows the articles.

30. Reed, Carroll E. Dialects of American English.
Foreword by Raven I. McDavid, Jr. Cleveland and New York:
The World Publishing Company, 1967. 119 pp. (Paper)
A discussion of American English based on data provided by the Linguistic Atlas and its various sectional divisions. The discussion covers the origins, the settlements,
and the expansion westward of the American language. A
selected bibliography is included as well as maps from the
linguistic sectional studies.

Literary Dialect

1. Ives, Sumner, "A Theory of Literary Dialect, "
Tulane Studies in English, II (1950), 137-182.
Ives's purpose in this article is to formulate principles by which the representation of American English dialects
in literature may be evaluated. The two major factors in the

development of his theory are the teachings of linguistic geography and the limitations of conventional orthography. He bases his analysis on the examination of actual practices of authors.

Ives defines dialect as the use in one locality of speech traits that may be individually found somewhere else and literary dialect as an author's attempt to represent in writing a speech that is restricted regionally, socially, or both. This representation may be by an occasional spelling change, or by attempting to represent all the grammatical, lexical, and phonetic peculiarities the author has observed. In addition, the writer of literary dialect must also represent unconventional morphology, local expressions, and local names for things. The investigator of literary dialect should have a concept of dialect which fits the facts of American English as they have been determined by research in the field. He must have a wide knowledge of both the variations and the consistencies which are present in American English and he must have an intensive knowledge of the distribution limits of the individual characteristics of this speech. The investigator must use a sufficiently large sample of the literary dialect to insure the consideration of all the pertinent data.

2.   Krapp, George Philip, "Literary Dialects," in The English Language in America. New York: The Century Company, 1925, I, 225-273.
A discussion of the dialects chosen for literary purposes through an examination of the details of speech used to produce the dialects. Krapp distinguishes three kinds of dialects--class dialect, foreign-mixed dialect, and local dialects--and discusses the dialect writing of such writers as James Russell Lowell, John Hay, Joel Chandler Harris, Bret Harte, Thomas Nelson Page, Ambrose E. Gonzales, and William Gilmore Simms.

3.   Riley, James Whitcomb, "Dialect in Literature," The Forum, XIV (September, 1892-February, 1893), 465-473.
Riley defines dialect as "any speech or vernacular outside the prescribed form of good English in its present state." It is something more than mere rude forms of speech and action. It is natural and human. The user of dialect must know not only the dialect itself but also the character of the people whose native tongue it is. Riley discusses the dialect writing of Richard Malcolm Johnston, Joel Chandler Harris, Thomas Nelson Page, James Russell Lowell, and Edward Eggleston, as examples of good dialect.

4. Williamson, Thames, "The Novelist's Use of Dialect," The Writer, XLVII (January, 1935), 3-5, 24, 40.
Williamson says that since the basic purpose of the novel is to arouse feeling in the reader, the language must be intelligible. Many times a familiar word or expression can be substituted for one unfamiliar without loss of effect. He advises the novelist to use clichés sparingly, to make careful use of misspellings and elisions, to allow different pronunciations for persons of different ages, and not to try to be consistent with dialect in conversation. Williamson concludes that the novelist wants flavor for his art but not scientific exactness. "Dialect is like garlic. A little of it is sometimes very fine, too much of it is horrible."

Analysis of Dialect in Literature

1. Creswell, Thomas J., "Literary Dialect in Nelson Algren's 'Never Come Morning,'" in Studies in Linguistics in Honor of Raven I. McDavid, Jr. General Editor, Lawrence M. Davis. University, Ala.: University of Alabama Press, 1972, pp. 29-40.
The characters in Never Come Morning are almost exclusively Polish-Americans. To indicate this, Creswell uses Polish surnames and in some cases Polish given names and nicknames. In moments of extreme stress some of the characters use their native language. To indicate first-generation characters, Algren omits the pronomial subject, future tense markers, and conjunctions. Other characteristics of the language include the omission of the article a, of the expletive it, of that in a series, of the infinitive sign to; failure to inflect the verb; the substitution of for for to and for for of; the use of the appended second person vocative; and of misplaced adverbs. There are a few indications of variations in pronunciation.

2. Davis, Lawrence M. "Literary Dialect in Milt Gross' 'Nize Baby,'" in Studies in Linguistics in Honor of Raven I. McDavid, Jr. General Editor, Lawrence M. Davis. University, Ala.: University of Alabama Press, 1972, pp. 41-47.
Davis says that Gross is inconsistent in his use of literary dialect, especially in spelling to indicate phonological aspects of the character's speech. For sounds that are readily adaptable to the Yiddish-English dialect, Gross has a tendency to substitute eye dialect. Gross is also inconsistent in syntax. He substitutes one word for another, omits pronouns

entirely, and makes changes in sentence structure. His characters sometimes put adverbials immediately after the verb, use non-parallel verb tenses, employ parallel tenses where they are not used in English, put verb phrases before noun phrases, place the object before the subject and verb when pronouns are used, and use malapropisms for humorous effect.

3. Evans, William. "French-English Literary Dialect in The Grandissimes," American Speech, XLV-XLVI (1970-1971), 210-222.
Evans discusses the phonology, the grammar, the sources of the dialect, the accuracy of the dialect, and the literary effectiveness of the French-English dialect as used by George W. Cable in The Grandissimes, a novel of the Creoles in Louisiana at the time of the official arrival of the Americans in 1803. He concludes that Cable represented the French-English dialect in "a reasonable, realistic manner," and that his changes in the dialect in the revised edition of 1883 were for simplicity and ease in reading. "It was an English, a French-flavored English, that could be useful and effective in linking like characters together, in differentiating contrasting characters, and in distinguishing different moods in a given character. And it formed a significant part of Cable's attempt to preserve something of a unique and valuable, but declining, culture and to make the world aware of it."

4. Foster, Charles W. The Phonology of the Conjure Tales of Charles W. Chesnutt. Publication of the American Dialect Society, Number 55 (April, 1971). 43 pp.
Guy S. Lowman's unpublished field records for the Linguistic Atlas of the Middle and South Atlantic States were used to establish the standard or author's phonology. Any word in The Conjure Woman spelled differently from the conventional spelling was considered important. Foster says that the author's own speech habits must be understood in evaluating literary dialect, and the writer of dialect must use a system of spelling that approximates the sound intended. The dialect of the characters should also represent the dialect of a certain social class in a certain region. Foster concludes that the dialect of Uncle Julius in The Conjure Tales is not a combination of forms taken from earlier dialect writers but is a product of Chesnutt's creative imagination, and that the dialect contributes to the reader's conception of the locale as well as to the era represented in the book. "It is far more than a record of speech that Chesnutt

might have heard, for in its manipulation and concentration, in its authenticity and balance, it becomes fused, in The Conjure Woman, into a work that has earned Chesnutt a place high in the ranks of Negro novelists and given him a place of esteem among writers of dialect fiction. "

5. Ives, Sumner, "Dialect Differentiation in the Stories of Joel Chandler Harris, " American Literature, XXVII (March, 1955), 88-96.
Ives says that many distinct speech patterns existed in Middle Georgia at the time Harris was writing and that Harris must have had a keen ear and an exact memory, for he was able to distinguish the various dialects to indicate social standing as well as the generation to which a character belonged. He says that social distinctions are shown by both the density and the choice of the nonstandard forms and that archaisms give an indication of the generation of the characters. Grammar and vocabulary of local speech can be shown with little difficulty but pronunciation is more difficult to represent and authors are apt to use only pronunciations that are socially indicative. Ives discusses Harris's representation of Negro speech in the Uncle Remus stories, which, he says, except for the use of Gullah by Daddy Jack, is hardly distinguishable from the rustic white speech except in density. He uses the speech of characters in Sister Jane to show how Harris differentiates white dialects. Ives concludes that Harris "handled the dialogue of his folk characters with skillful discrimination. "

6. Ives, Sumner, "The Phonology of the Uncle Remus Stories, " Publications of the American Dialect Society, No. 22 (November, 1954).
An interpretation of the phonology of the Uncle Remus stories derived from a study of the spellings which Joel Chandler Harris used to represent it. The study is based on a dissertation, directed by E. Bagby Atwood at the University of Texas, on The Negro Dialect of the Uncle Remus Stories. For interpretation and verification of the dialect Ives used the field records of the Linguistic Atlas of the United States and Canada. He also traced the various characteristics of the Uncle Remus dialect through all the available field records for the Southeast. In making the analysis, Ives assumed that every word which does not have the dictionary spelling should be included. From the analysis, Ives concludes that Harris developed literary dialect from "genuine materials, " and that the folk speech of the plantation Negro has been successfully used as a literary medium and

that both the speech and the fictional character of Uncle Remus have been created from authentic raw materials.

7.   Lowenherz, Robert J. , "The Beginning of 'Huckleberry Finn, '" American Speech, XXXVIII (February-December, 1963), 196-201.

Lowenherz shows through an analysis of the language of the first paragraph of only 108 words that Mark Twain "firmly establishes the vernacular speech of the narrator Huck, characterizes him, enunciates one of the major themes of the novel, provides a frame of reference for the action, and even works in some free advertisement for his earlier novel, The Adventures of Tom Sawyer. "

8.   McGuire, William Joseph, Jr.   A Study of Florida Cracker Dialect Based Chiefly on the Prose Works of Marjorie Kinnan Rawlings.   M. A. thesis, University of Florida, 1939.   Typed copy.

A study of the dialect in the novels and stories of Marjorie Kinnan Rawlings with field work of conferences with Mrs. Rawlings and with Cracker informants. Also used were data from works on Florida history and census records; word lists and studies of other Cracker dialects; and standard philological works of reference. The seven chapters are concerned with the historical background of the dialect as well as with vocabulary, phonology, morphology, and syntax. There is also a bibliography of works related to the study of Cracker dialects. McGuire concludes that although Mrs. Rawlings lacks linguistic training, her handling of the central Florida Cracker dialect is, by and large, accurate and thorough.

9.   Pound, Louise, "The Dialect of Cooper's Leather-Stocking," American Speech, II (September, 1927), 479-488.

Pound says that Cooper handles dialect "more or less amateurishly," with results that are equal to those of his contemporaries but not equal to the dialect of Scott, from whom he learned. The Deerslayer, the volume Cooper wrote last, is most heavily weighted with dialect, while The Prairie, which he wrote while in Europe, has the least amount of dialect. Pound analyzes the dialect of Leather-Stocking from the standpoints of pronunciation, grammatical forms, and vocabulary. She says that non-standard pronunciation plays a larger role in his dialect than do faults in grammar or in misuse of words. The most frequent variation from the standard in pronunciation is the substitution of ar for er, ir. Next in number are examples of fluctuation between e and i.

Other non-standard pronunciations include the use of on- for
un-, secondary accent on the last syllable resulting in lengthening of the vowel, and vowel weakening of the final syllable.
Consonant changes are fewer but they include consonant substitution and consonant loss of w, f, r, l, s, d. Dialect
forms in grammar include unusual forms of the plural of
nouns; pair as plural; possessive their'n, our'n, his'n,
your'n; them as a demonstrative; confusion of nominative and
accusative; certain dialectal prepositions and adverbs; and
wrong use of verbs. Pound says that Leather-Stocking's vocabulary is narrow and hard-worked. She concludes that
Cooper is probably at his worst in his use of dialect, but
since it is free of slang and simplified spelling, it has more
dignity than more modern slang and will probably remain intelligible longer.

    10. Randall, Dale B. J. , "Dialect in the Verse of
'The Hoosier Poet, '" American Speech, XXXV (February-
December, 1960), 36-50.
    An analysis of Riley's dialect based on opinions con-
cerning Riley's dialect, his method of work, his own comments and poems, and the nature of Hoosier speech. Randall uses five poems from Farm-Rhymes as the basis of his
analysis of Riley's dialect, which he considers from the
standpoints of pronunciation, morphology and syntax, and vocabulary. He concludes that the most characteristic features
of the pronunciation are the dropping of final g and of initial
a, the addition of a at the beginning of present participles,
the -er or -or endings for words ending in -ow, although
Riley's practice is not consistent. In morphology and syntax,
the nonstandard forms include variant verb forms, subject-
verb disagreement, and double negative. A comparison of
Riley's vocabulary with the glossary of Hoosierisms compiled by O. W. Henley reveals some of the words used by
Riley, and in the correspondence of uneducated nineteenth-
century Indianians one may find nearly all of Riley's eye
dialect words. Riley's dialect has also been substantiated by
the work of modern scholars.

    11. Schrock, Earl F. , Jr. , "An Examination of the
Dialect in This Day and Time," Tennessee Folklore Society
Bulletin, XXXVII (June, 1971), 31-39. Reprinted in Voices
from the Hills. Selected Readings of Southern Appalachia.
Edited by Robert J. Higgs and Ambrose N. Manning. New
York: Frederick Ungar Publishing Company, 1975, pp. 460-
473.
    Schrock examines the dialect in This Day and Time
(1930), a regional novel by Anne W. Armstrong, set in

Sullivan County, Tennessee, in the 1920's, and using mainly the speech of the uneducated mountaineer. He discusses vocabulary; phonetic spelling used to reflect the pronunciations, especially of vowels; the verbs and adjectives peculiar to the Southern Appalachians; the use of comparative and superlative suffixes; redundancy, particularly with personal pronouns; use of where as a pronoun; phrases of exclamation and other stock expressions. Schrock says that Mrs. Armstrong strives so hard to represent Appalachian speech accurately that sometimes she sacrifices effectiveness to exactness. He also comments on the fact that since language constantly changes, many of the forms Mrs. Armstrong uses are no longer in existence.

12. Wright, Nathalie, "The East Tennessee Background of Sidney Lanier's Tiger-Lilies," American Literature, XIX (March, 1947-January, 1948), 127-138.
In her discussion of Tiger-Lilies, Wright says that Lanier's novel is one of the earliest treatments of the Southern mountaineers and their speech, and one of the earliest authoritative records of the language of southern Appalachia. "Far more naturalistic than the caricaturing of his contemporary George Washington Harris, it equals in all but extent the later achievement of Mary Noailles Murfree." Wright says that Lanier paid strict attention to the syntax, pronunciation, and vocabulary of his characters. His syntax is archaic and redundant. Such words as "hit," "ax," "afore," "for to," "of a," "ary" are used. Multiple negatives are employed as well as weak preterits, indiscriminate use of prefixes, adverbs from adjectives, verbs from adverbs, interchangeable vowels, and idioms.

Recordings of American English Dialects

Americans Speaking by John Muri and Raven I. McDavid, Jr. Lp. recordings of set passages and free discourse read by speakers from six dialect areas in the United States. Accompanied by a pamphlet with texts of passages and a checklist for listening. National Council of Teachers of English, 1967. Stock No. 24306.

"Ever'body says words different," said Ivy. "Arkansas folks says 'em different, and Oklahomy folks says 'em different. And we seen a lady from Massachusetts, an' she said 'em differentest of all. Couldn' hardly make out what she was sayin'."

--John Steinbeck, <u>The Grapes of Wrath</u>. New York: Modern Library Edition, p. 184.

CHAPTER II

NEW ENGLAND DIALECTS

Historical Background

In A Word Geography of the Eastern States, [31] Hans
Kurath says that the Linguistic Atlas data show three broad
dialect areas along the Atlantic coast: the North, the Midland, and the South. The North comprises New England,
the inland North, the Hudson Valley, and Metropolitan New
York. The Midland is divided into North Midland, Pennsylvania and Northern West Virginia; and South Midland, the
Shenandoah Valley and the Southern Appalachians. The South
consists of Delmarva, the Virginia Piedmont, Northeastern
North Carolina, Cape Fear and Peedee Valleys, and the South
Carolina Low Country.

New England has two major dialect areas, Eastern and
Western. [32] The Eastern area has Boston as its center and
extends from the Atlantic seaboard to the Connecticut River
Valley in Massachusetts, including the Plymouth Area, the
Narragansett Bay Area, the New Hampshire Bay and the Mer-
rimack Valley Area, Maine and New Hampshire, with a dis-
tinct speech in Northern Maine, the New London area, and
Worcester County and the Upper Connecticut Valley. Western
New England includes the Lower Connecticut Valley and the
Long Island Sound west of the Connecticut River. Carroll E.
Reed says that as the inhabitants of coastal New England were
sea-going people, they played an important role in the settle-
ments around San Francisco, the lower Columbia River, and
Puget Sound. [33] He concludes: "Words of general occurrence
on the East Coast are usually common also in the Pacific
Northwest." See David W. Reed, "Eastern Dialect Words in
California," page 151.

New England was populated largely by people from the eastern and southern parts of England. Western New England had a number of emigrants from the area north and northwest of London, as well as settlers from northern England. There were also Scotch-Irish, but they settled along the frontiers. [34]

The dialect of Eastern New England is characterized by distinguishing the vowel in "hot" and "top" from the broad a in "father." But the broad a is used in "pass," "fast," and "grass," while "r" is dropped except before vowels, as in "car" and "hard." [35] The dialect of New York is largely confined to the Metropolitan area. The "r" is generally also lost but "curl" and "third" become "coil" and "thoid" in common speech. [36] Western New England has contributed more to the speech of the northern United States than has Eastern New England. The speech of Upstate New York is also derived from that of New England, but some of the features peculiar to eastern New England, such as the loss of post-vocalic /r/ in beard, hard, board, or the low front vowel of /a/ in half, pass, aunt, survive only in certain localities. [37]

Studies in New England Dialect

1. Bennett, Jacob. "George Savary Wasson and the Dialect of Kittery Point, Maine," American Speech, XLIX (Spring-Summer, 1974), 54-66.
An analysis of the phonological, morphological, and lexical characteristics of Wasson's Kittery Point dialect to determine how accurately it represents the original. Bennett checked his results with the three major volumes based on the Linguistic Atlas records and against the speech of three aged Kittery residents. The items that could be verified offer strong proof of Wasson's representation and indicate that the others Wasson used must also be largely representative of the dialect of the folk speech of Kittery Point, York County, Maine, in the latter part of the nineteenth century. Bennett says that Wasson used a systematic and consistent orthography to reproduce the dialectal distinctions of sound; he was careful in gathering morphological, lexical, and phonological data; and his dialectal forms correlate with a number of relevant ones in the Linguistic Atlas and with those in the speech of the native informants. He says that there is nothing in Wasson that contradicts the Atlas findings but that Wasson includes thirty-eight features that agree with the Atlas. The informants offer about the same degree of corroboration as does the Atlas.

2. Bloch, Bernard. "Postvocalic r in New England Speech, A Study in American Dialect Geography," in Readings in American Dialectology. Edited by Harold B. Allen and Gary N. Underwood. New York: Appleton-Century-Crofts, 1971, pp. 196-199. Reprinted from Actes du quartième Congrès internationale de linguistes. Copenhagen: Munksgaard, 1939, pp. 195-199.

The material for this study, taken from records of the Linguistic Atlas of New England, is concerned with the distribution of forms with and without r in present-day New England speech and with the observable drifts in the local dialects of the region. Bloch says that from the geographical distribution of r in words like work, three facts are obvious: Western New England speech pronounces the r, while in eastern New England the r is usually silent; no clear boundary can be drawn between the two sections; in both sections, especially in central and southeastern New England, the usage of many individual speakers is inconsistent. Although the pronunciation with r is the prevailing type in the western third of New England, in central and eastern New England there are several "speech islands" where the treatment of r is different from the practice of the section as a whole. Only in the immediate neighborhood of Boston and in the greater part of New Hampshire and Maine is the so-called Eastern pronunciation universal. Bloch says that the Linguistic Atlas of New England also provides evidence that the dialect is in the process of change. In some areas, the pronunciation with r is growing more general and in other areas there is a gradual disappearance of r.

3. Eby, Cecil D., Jr. "Americanisms in the Down-East Fiction of George S. Wasson," American Speech, XXXVII (February-December, 1962), 249-254.

Eby says that Wasson's stories seem to have as their main purpose the accurate recording of colorful Maine speech and in many of his stories the narration is carried entirely by the conversation of the Maine characters. The dialect is thus one of the most durable achievements of the writing. Eby includes a list of sixty-eight words and phrases apparently first recorded by Wasson and checked with their appearance in the OED, DA, DAE, and ADD. The study is based on the following books by Wasson: Cap'n Simeon's Store, 1903; The Green Shay, 1905; and Home from the Sea, 1908.

4. Lowell, James Russell. "Introduction" to The Biglow Papers, First Series (1849), and "Introduction" to The Biglow Papers, Second Series (1866), in The Complete Writ-

ings of James Russell Lowell. New York: AMS Press,
Inc., 1966. Vol. X, pp. 31-58; Vol. XI, pp. 5-99.

In his introduction to The Biglow Papers, First Series,
Lowell lays down seven general rules to guide the reader of
Yankee dialect: The genuine Yankee never gives the rough
sound to r; he seldom sounds the final g and d; he omits the
h in such words as while and when; he sometimes pronounces
a as the e in hev for have and sometimes as the broad sound
as in father; to the sound of ou, he prefixes an e; au in such
words as daughter and slaughter, he pronounces as ah; "To
the dish thus seasoned add a drawl ad libitum."

In the introduction to The Biglow Papers, Second Series, Lowell traces many of the features of the New England
dialect to its use in English literature--pronunciation, words
and phrases, contractions, etc.--and argues for simplicity,
directness, precision, and force in American writing through
the use of the popular idiom, for "it is only from its roots
in the living generations of men that a language can be rein-
forced with fresh vigor for its needs."

5. Thomas, C. K. "The Phonology of New England
English," in Readings in American Dialectology. Edited by
Harold B. Allen and Gary N. Underwood. New York: Apple-
ton-Century-Crofts, 1971, pp. 57-66. Reprinted from Speech
Monographs, XXVIII (1961), 223-32.

A study based on the speech of 1,226 speakers, most
of them college students, representing every county in six
New England states, their distribution roughly in proportion
to the population of these counties, to determine the predominant forms in words of divided usage and to determine the
geographical areas in which the predominance of certain
forms differs from the predominance in other areas within
the region.

6. Thomas, C. K. "The Place of New York City in
American Linguistic Geography," Quarterly Journal of Speech,
XXXIII (1947), 314-320.

Thomas says that the speech of New England east of
the Connecticut River is part of the coastal variety that extended in colonial times from Maine to Georgia. Later the
western type developed largely west of the Connecticut River,
but "New England speech" is the speech of eastern New England although there are differences within the area. Thomas
lists the characteristic features of eastern New England
speech, traces the history of the settlements of the New York
City area, and gives an analysis of the pronunciation of New
York City speech based on his own records of the speech of

500 persons in New York City, 500 in adjoining counties of New York State, and 200 in southwestern Connecticut and the river counties of New Jersey.

7. White, E. B. "Maine Speech," in One Man's Meat. New and enlarged edition. New York and London: Harper and Brothers, 1939-1944, pp. 190-193. First published October, 1940.

A discussion of the peculiarities of Maine speech--in the meaning of words, in pronunciation, and in grammar-- with examples to illustrate each.

New England Dialect in Literature

Thomas Chandler HALIBURTON (1796-1865) a native of Nova Scotia, created the character of Sam Slick, a Yankee clock peddler. One writer says: "It is a little singular, but it is true, that scarcely any native writer has succeeded better in giving what is termed the true 'Yankee dialect,' than a foreigner, an Englishman, Judge Haliburton of Nova Scotia."[38]

Works:

The Clockmaker; or, The Sayings and Doings of Sam Slick, 1837.

The Attaché; or Sam Slick in England, 1843.

Harriet Beecher STOWE (1811-1896) was born in Litchfield, Connecticut. When she was twenty-one, she moved with her family to Cincinnati, where her father served as the first president of Lane Theological Seminary. Three years later, she married Calvin Stowe, a member of the Lane faculty. In 1850, the Stowe family moved to the East and there Stowe taught in Bowdoin and in Andover. Shortly after going to Bowdoin, Mrs. Stowe wrote Uncle Tom's Cabin, published as a book in 1852, and Dred, 1856, but it was her stories of prewar New England that are her best work. In writing these books, Mrs. Stowe said, "I have tried to make my mind as still and passive as a looking glass, or a mountain lake, and then to give you merely the images reflected there. I desire that you should see the characteristic persons of those times, and hear them talk."[39]

Works:

Oldtown Folks. Boston: Fields, Osgood and Company, 1869. 608 pp. Concerned with South Natick.

The Pearl of Orr's Island. A Story of the Coast of Maine. Boston: Houghton, Mifflin and Company, 1862. Republished, Ridgewood, N.J.: The Gregg Press, 1967. 402 pp. Kennebec Island life.

Sam Lawson's Oldtown Fireside Stories. Boston: Houghton, Mifflin and Company, 1872. Republished, Ridgewood, N.J.: The Gregg Press, 1967. 287 pp. Fifteen stories.

Poganuc People, 1878. Laid in Litchfield, Connecticut.

James Russell LOWELL (1819-1891) was born in Cambridge, Massachusetts. He graduated from Harvard in 1838, received a law degree from Harvard in 1840, but turned to writing instead. When he was thirty-seven, he succeeded Longfellow as Smith Professor of Modern Languages at Harvard. In 1857, he became editor of the Atlantic Monthly and in 1862 editor of the North American Review. He later served as Ambassador to Spain and Ambassador to England. The Biglow Papers, First Series, was written to protest the Mexican War. The Second Series offers comments on issues related to the Civil War.

Works:

The Biglow Papers, First Series, 1849, and The Biglow Papers, Second Series, 1866, in The Complete Writings of James Russell Lowell. New York: AMS Press, Inc., 1966. Vol. X, 220 pp. Vol. XI, 324 pp.

Rose Terry COOKE (1827-1892) was born on a farm near Hartford, Connecticut. She was educated in rural schools and at Hartford Seminary.

Works:

Root-Bound, 1885.

Huckleberries Gathered from New England Hills, 1891. Includes "Old Miss Todd," "The Town and Country Mouse," and "Freedom Wheeler's Controversy with Providence."

Rowland Evans ROBINSON (1833-1900), a blind Vermont Quaker, well-known in his day for his stories of Vermont at the middle of the century, lived in Farrisburg, Vermont. In the "Introductory Note" to Danvis Folks, Robinson says that this book was written to record "the manners, customs, and speech in vogue fifty or sixty years ago in certain parts of New England.... Though the dialect is yet spoken in almost its original quaintness, abounding in odd similes and figures of speech, it is passing away; so that one may look forward to the time when a Yankee may not be known by his speech, unless perhaps he shall speak a little better English than some of his neighbors."

Works:

Uncle Elisha's Shop: Life in a Corner of Yankeeland, 1887.

Danvis Folks. Boston: Houghton, Mifflin and Company, 1894. 349 pp.

A Danvis Pioneer, 1900.

Sam Lovel's Boy with Forest and Stream Fables. Foreword by John Spargo. Introduction by S. Foster Damon, 1901, 1936. Reprinted by Books for Libraries Press, 1971. 255 pp.

Sam Lovel's Camps and Other Stories. Includes In the Green Wood. Foreword by Duane Leroy Robinson. Introduction by Arthur Wallace Peach, 1934. Reprinted by Books for Libraries Press, 1971. 255 pp.

Sarah Orne JEWETT (1849-1909) was born in the village of South Berwick, Maine. Her formal schooling was irregular, but she read widely in her father's library and learned about the people of the area by traveling with her father, a country doctor, as he visited his patients in the fishing villages and on upland farms. Willa Cather says of Jewett's writing: "She had not only the eye, she had the ear. From childhood she must have treasured up those pithy bits of local speech, of native idiom, which enrich and enliven her pages. The language her people speak to each other is a native tongue. No writer can invent it. It is made in the hard school of experience, in communities where language has been undisturbed long enough to take on colour and character from the nature and experience of the people. "40

Works:

Deephaven, 1877. A collection of stories and sketches about life in a Maine village. 255 pp.

A Country Doctor, 1884. Boston: Houghton, Mifflin Company, 1912. 351 pp.

Tales of New England, 1894. Reprinted by Books for Libraries Press, 1970. 276 pp. Eight stories.

The Country of the Pointed Firs and Other Stories. Selected and arranged with a preface by Willa Cather. Garden City, N. Y.: Doubleday and Company, Inc., 1954. Doubleday Anchor Books. Twelve stories. First published in 1896.

Mary E. Wilkins FREEMAN (1852-1930) was born in Randolph, a village in eastern Massachusetts. She lived there and in Brattleboro, Vermont, where her father kept a store. She spent the year 1870-1871 at Mt. Holyoke Female Seminary. After the death of her parents in 1883, she returned to her native village to live. This village and the country around it furnished the materials for her early stories. In 1902, she married Dr. Charles M. Freeman and moved to Metuchen, New Jersey. From 1883 to 1918, she published over thirty volumes of fiction.

Works:

A Humble Romance and Other Stories. New York: Harper and Brothers, 1887. 436 pp. Contains twenty-eight stories, including "On the Walpole Road. "

A New England Nun and Other Stories. Contains twenty-four stories including "The Revolt of Mother, " first printed in Harper's New Monthly Magazine, September, 1890. New York: Harper and Brothers, 1891. 468 pp. Reprinted by The Gregg Press, Inc., 1967.

George Savary WASSON (1855-1932), artist and author, was born in Groveland, Massachusetts. He was educated at Medford High School and at private institutions. He took a three-year course at the Royal Würtemberg Art School. He built a house at Kittery Point, Maine, 1889, so that he could study the sea. He is buried at Bangor, Maine.

Works:

Cap'n Simeon's Store, 1903.

The Green Shay, 1906.

Home from the Sea, 1908. Reprinted by Books for Libraries Press, 1970. Contains about thirty stories.

Alice BROWN (1857-1948) was born on a farm in Hampton Falls, New Hampshire. She attended Robinson Seminary in Exeter. She published twenty novels, several volumes of short stories, two volumes of poems, a few plays, two biographies, and a study of Robert Louis Stevenson in collaboration with Louise Imogene Guiney. Her play, Children of Earth, 1916, won a $10,000 prize. She had an especial ear for her native dialect.

Works:

Meadow-Grass: Tales of New England Life. Boston: Houghton, Mifflin and Company, 1895, 315 pp.

Tiverton Tales. Boston: Houghton, Mifflin and Company, 1899. Republished by The Gregg Press, Inc., 1967. 339 pp. Twelve stories.

The Country Road, 1906. Boston: Houghton, Mifflin and Company. Republished by The Gregg Press, Inc., 1968. 341 pp. Thirteen stories.

Daniel L. CADY (1861-1934), wrote of rural Vermont in dialect verse that one critic says is equal to any dialect verse in America with the exception of the dialect poems of Lowell.

Works:

Rhymes of Vermont Rural Life, First Series, 1919. 279 pp. Contains 107 pieces with 114 "mentions of Vermont localities. " Second Series, 1922, 280 pp. Contains 107 pieces with "seventy-seven mentions of Vermont localities. " Third Series, 1926. 255 pp. Contains 107 pieces with "sixty-nine mentions of Vermont locations. "

Eugene O'NEILL (1888-1953). For a short biography of O'Neill, see pages 103-4.

Works:

Desire under the Elms. Produced by Provincetown Playhouse, Greenwich Village Theatre, New York, November 11, 1924.

Sidney HOWARD (1891-1939). For a short biography of Howard, see page 163.

Works:

Ned McCobb's Daughter. First produced in New York by the Theatre Guild, on November 22, 1926. In The Play's the Thing. Edited by Fred B. Millett and Gerald Eades Bentley. New York: Appleton-Century-Crofts, 1936, 1964, pp. 325-362.

"Dialect must seduce the eye to reach the ear and be orchestrated in the brain. It must tantalize without irritating, and defer without frustrating. It must carry a visual promise to the reader that what he does not instantly recognize can be deciphered with ease and will be rewarded with pleasure. The reader must be cued into making what he thinks is his own special and private discovery--a discovery of delight which, he suspects, neither the character nor the author fully appreciates. "

--Leo Rosten. "Preface: The Confessions of Mr. Parkhill, " The Return of H*Y*M*A*N K*A*P*L*A*N. New York: Harper & Row, Publishers, 1938, 1959, p. 14.

CHAPTER III

MIDDLE ATLANTIC DIALECTS

Historical Background

The Middle Atlantic area includes all of New Jersey except the most northern part; the southeastern third of Pennsylvania and all of Delaware. In Maryland the speech is mixed. Some of it is Middle Atlantic and some Southern. The District of Columbia, its Virginia suburbs, and the eastern shore from Ocean City, Maryland, to Cape Charles, Virginia, are largely Middle Atlantic in speech. [41] The Midland is not a uniform speech area. Its chief sub-areas are Eastern Pennsylvania and West Jersey, the main areas of Pennsylvania German; Western Pennsylvania and Northern West Virginia; the Southern Appalachians and the Blue Ridge south of the James River. The Philadelphia area, consisting of Eastern Pennsylvania and West Jersey, and the Pittsburgh area of Western Pennsylvania constitute North Midland. The Southern Appalachians and the Blue Ridge south of the James are known as the South Midland. West Midland consists of the Pittsburgh area and the South Midland. [42]

The most interesting dialect of the Mid-Atlantic area is the Pennsylvania German-English dialect, the oldest surviving foreign language colony in the United States. Its history of continued use in a particular area goes back to 1683, when immigrants from the southwestern part of Germany began to settle in Pennsylvania. By 1775 there were about 90,000 Germans, largely from the Rhenish Palatinate. [43] Laird says that the refugees to this country in the seventeenth and eighteenth centuries include "Reformed Lutherans from Württemberg and Alsace, Moravians from the Palatinate, Schwenfelders and Amish and Mennonites, all somewhat identifiable both in Europe and America."[44]

39

These Germans developed a language of their own that became known as Pennsylvania German or Pennsylvania Dutch. It was a combination of their various dialects with a mixture of English words and constructions. ("There was perhaps a distinctive PaG dialect as early as 1800. "[45]) It is a language still spoken by about 25 per cent of the inhabitants of Lehigh, Lebanon, and Berks counties in Pennsylvania and understood by 60 to 65 per cent of the people. [46] Marckwardt attributes its persistence to the isolation of such religious sects as the Amish and Menonnites. Laird says: "According to recent estimates, some 300,000 Americans feel more comfortable speaking Pennsylvania Dutch than speaking English, and a considerably larger number use the language readily. "[47]

According to C. M. Wise, Pennsylvania German "possesses no rounded front sounds such as High German possesses, contains no aspirate explosive, i. e. , no aspirate [p, t, k], except initially before a vowel; contains no voiced plosives at all, i. e. , no [b, d, g]; and has no voiced fricative except [γ], and [β], so that there is no [v] (except as a member of the [β] phoneme), and no consistent use of [z]. As will be seen, these same conditions as to aspiration and voicing apply, with reasonable uniformity, to the speaking of English by the Pennsylvania German people. "[48] The Pennsylvania German contains many loan words from English that are pronounced very much as if they were German. In questions and in some declarative sentences, the voice rises on the stressed word or syllable preceding the word or last syllable. [49]

Studies in Middle Atlantic Dialects

1.   Bronstein, Arthur J.   "Let's Take Another Look at New York City Speech, " American Speech, XXXVII (February, 1962), 13-26.
Bronstein discusses four general items of information that he thinks useful for understanding New York City speech: the New York City speech area is a separate dialect area and not a part of the New England dialect area; in order to understand the dialect, the adjacent geographic areas must be combined with the city into a single speech community; substandard and foreign speech forms are not the speech commonly heard in New York City; certain conclusions about the substandard forms of New York City speech commonly found in textbooks are not justified.   Bronstein presents his

impressions of New York City speech after studying the
speech of students at Queens College, but he points out the
need for further study.

2.   Buffington, Albert F.   "Pennsylvania German:
Its Relation to Other German Dialects," American Speech,
XIV (1939), 276-286.
Pennsylvania Dutch or Pennsylvania German is a
blend of the several German dialects used by the early German settlers of Pennsylvania with the speech of the Palatinate predominating.   Buffington says that English had considerable influence on the syntax and vocabulary of the dialect
but little influence on the phonology and morphology.   He
points out some of the phonetic phenomena found in Pennsylvania German but not found in other German dialects, some
of the phonetic peculiarities Pennsylvania German has in common with the dialects of the eastern half of the Palatinate,
the peculiarities of Pennsylvania German morphology, examples of Alemannic influence on Pennsylvania German morphology, and examples of English influence on the syntax and vocabulary of Pennsylvania German.

3.   The German Language in America, A Symposium.
Edited with an Introduction by Glenn G. Gilbert.   Austin,
Texas: University of Texas Press, 1971.   217 pp.
A collection of the papers and discussions of the
Tenth Germanic Language Symposium, held at the University
of Texas at Austin, November 18-20, 1968.   The nine papers
concern not only the German language in various sections of
the United States but also discussions of German folklore and
proposals for the further study of the German language in
this country.   Two of the papers are of particular concern
here: "The Word Geography of Pennsylvania German: Extent and Causes," and "German in Virginia and West Virginia."

4.   Seifert, Lester W. J.   "The Word Geography of
Pennsylvania: Extent and Causes," in The German Language
in America.   Edited with an Introduction by Glenn W. Gilbert.
Austin, Texas: University of Texas Press, 1971, pp. 14-42.
An account of studies of Pennsylvania, of the history
of German settlements in the United States, of the areas in
Europe from which the settlers came, of the process of leveling of the various dialects, and of the eight main categor-
ies of regional distribution.

5.   Tucker, R. Whitney.   "Notes on the Philadelphia
Dialect," American Speech, XIX (1944), 37-42.

A discussion of the characteristic features of the
Philadelphia dialect, of the features it shares with other di-
alects and of those in which it differs from other dialects.
According to Tucker, this dialect is an eastern variety of
General American in which final and preconsonantal r is gen-
erally pronounced.

6. Wise, Claude Merton. "Pennsylvania German
('Pennsylvania Dutch'), " in Applied Phonetics. Englewood
Cliffs, N. J.: Prentice-Hall, 1957, pp. 403-410.
The Pennsylvania German dialect of English is the
English spoken by people of German extraction in the counties of Northampton, Lehigh, Berks, Lebanon, Lancaster,
York, Schuylkill, and Dauphin in southeastern Pennsylvania
and to some extent in adjacent parts of Maryland, Virginia,
and West Virginia. The main period of German colonization
in Pennsylvania took place between 1683 and 1734. The people, largely from Germany and Switzerland, while in Europe
spoke dialects different from standard High German and to
some extent from each other. In Pennsylvania their separa-
tion from Germany and Switzerland caused their dialects to
fuse into a single dialect. This dialect contains a long list
of English loan words pronounced in the main as if they were
German words. When the Pennsylvania German speaks English, he uses loan words from the German, modified English
words, and some German loan words. Thus there are four
levels of speech recognized in the Pennsylvania German area:
Pennsylvania German itself; Pennsylvania German dialect of
English as spoken by the less literate people; English containing German idioms; and Standard General American English. The main features of the Pennsylvania German dialect
used by the less educated members of the population include
peculiarities in pronunciation, intonation, and stress.

Middle Atlantic Dialects in Literature

Edward Noyes WESTCOTT (1847-1898) was born in
Syracuse, New York, where he lived most of his life. Bank-
ing was his main occupation. David Harum was completed
in the latter part of 1896 but Westcott died before the book
was published.

Works:

David Harum. New York: D. Appleton and Company,
1898. 392 pp. Dialect of rural New York.

Helen R. MARTIN (1868-1939) was born in Lancaster, Pennsylvania, and educated at Swarthmore and at Radcliffe. She wrote short stories and novels, mainly about the Pennsylvania Dutch.

Works:

Tillie, a Mennonite Maid: A Story of the Pennsylvania Dutch. With illustrations by Florence Scovel Shinn. The Century Company, 1904. 336 pp. Republished by The Gregg Press, 1968.

Sabina: A Story of the Amish, 1905.

Martha of the Mennonite Country, 1915.

Yoked with a Lamb, and Other Stories, 1930. Reprinted by Books for Libraries Press, 1971. 325 pp. Ten stories.

Elsie SINGMASTER (1879-1958) was born in Schuylkill Haven, Pennsylvania, where her father was preaching. After four years, her family moved to Allentown. She attended Cornell and then Radcliffe. She graduated in 1907 and five years later married Harold Lewars, a musician, and went to live in Harrisburg. In 1915, Lewars died and she returned to her father's house in Gettysburg, where he was president of the theological seminary. Singmaster wrote seven novels and more than two hundred short stories.

Works:

Katy Gaumer, 1910, 1915.

"The Belsnickel," in America through the Short Story. Edited by Bryllion Fagin. Boston: Little, Brown and Company, 1937, pp. 89-99. First published in Century Magazine, January, 1911, and later embodied in Katy Gaumer.

Bred in the Bone. Mennonite Tales, 1925.

The Magic Mirror. Boston: Houghton Mifflin Company, 1934. 284 pp.

Thames Ross WILLIAMSON (1894-   ). For a short biographical account of Williamson, see page 80.

Works:

D Is for Dutch, 1934. A dialect story of the Pennsylvania Dutch.

Thomas WOLFE (1900-1938). For a biographical account of Wolfe, see page 81.

Works:

"Only the Dead Know Brooklyn," in From Death to Morning, 1932. Reprinted in The Portable Thomas Wolfe. Edited by Maxwell Geismar. New York: The Viking Press, 1948, pp. 636-643.

Records in Pennsylvania Dutch Dialect

J. W. Frey. Folksongs of the Pennsylvania Dutch. Nelson Cornell Custom Records, Inc. Distributed by the Pennsylvania Dutch Folklore Society, Lancaster, Pennsylvania.

"... The South is linguistically the most diverse part of the nation; Southerners are not trapped into the fallacy of a uniform and monolithic standard, but cheerfully recognize that Richmonders and Atlantans, Charlestonians and Orleanians, Montgomeryites and Nashvillians can speak standard English in their diverse local accents. Furthermore, despite the public hokum of Southern aristocracy, the South--more than any other region--still maintains something like the aristocratic attitude in language, by which one shifts not only vocabulary and pronunciation, but even grammar, according to the audience. And Southerners, it would seem from informal observation, have the greatest variation between the formal and informal usage of educated speakers. In a nation that cringes too often under the glib criticism of the overliterate uneducated, ... it would seem that the South has an unusual opportunity to provide the intellectual leadership that will make possible a more intelligent and effective program of teaching the English language. "

--Raven I. McDavid, Jr., "Dialectology: Where Linguistics Meets the People, " The Emory University Quarterly, XXIII (Winter, 1967), 219.

CHAPTER IV

SOUTHERN DIALECTS

The Southern speech area of the eastern states as
determined by Hans Kurath from materials in the collection
of the Linguistic Atlas and presented in A Word Geography
of the Eastern United States includes five sections extending
from southern Delaware and the eastern shore of Maryland
and Virginia to east Texas, probably to the valley of the
Brazos River. Wise includes the cities of Beaumont, Gal-
veston, and Houston in the southern area. [50] This study also
includes the southern Appalachian area, the Ozarks, the
states of Alabama, Arkansas, Florida, Georgia, Louisiana,
Mississippi, Oklahoma, Tennessee, southern Missouri and
Kansas, and eastern Texas. In general, the divisions are
as follows: the Southern lowlander, the mountaineer, the
Negro as represented by both Whites and Negroes, and
special groups such as the Gullah and the Louisiana French
Creoles and Cajuns.

Bibliographies of Southern Speech

1.   Berrey, Lester V.   "Southern Mountain Dialect, "
American Speech, XV (February, 1940), 53-54.

2.   Kennedy, Arthur G.   "American Sectional Dialects, " in Bibliography of Writings on the English Language,
from the Beginning of Printing to the End of 1922.   Cambridge, Mass. :   Harvard University Press, 1927; reissued
New York: Hafner, 1961, pp. 413-416.

3.   McMillan, James B.   Annotated Bibliography of
Southern American English. Coral Gables, Fla. : University of Miami Press, 1971.   173 pp.

4. McMillan, James B. "Southern Speech," in A Bibliographical Guide to the Study of Southern Literature. Edited by Louis D. Rubin, Jr. Baton Rouge, La.: Louisiana State University Press, 1969, pp. 128-134.

5. Pederson, Lee A. An Annotated Bibliography of Southern Speech. Hopeville, Ga.: Southeastern Educational Laboratory, 1968. 47 pp. (Paper)

6. Randolph, Vance, and George P. Wilson. Down in the Holler: A Gallery of Ozark Folk Speech. Norman, Okla.: University of Oklahoma Press, 1953, pp. 303-314.

7. Woodbridge, Hensley C. "A Tentative Bibliography of Kentucky Speech," PADS, No. 30 (November, 1958), 17-37.

Studies of Southern Dialects

1. Brooks, Cleanth. "The English Language in the South," in A Southern Treasury of Life and Literature. Edited by Stark Young. New York: Scribner's, 1937, pp. 350-358. Reprinted in Contemporary Southern Prose. Edited by R. C. Beatty and W. P. Fidler. New York: Heath, 1940, pp. 49-57; A Vanderbilt Miscellany. Edited by R. C. Beatty. Nashville: Vanderbilt University Press, 1944, pp. 179-187. Reprinted in The Literature of the South. Edited by R. C. Beatty, F. C. Watkins, T. D. Young. New York: Scott-Foresman, 1952, pp. 745-750; Second edition, 1968, pp. 705-710.
Brooks says that Southern English is not a corrupt form of standard English and its origin is not determined by Negro influence. It represents a form of English older than that found in standard British today. Some Southern pronunciations represent forms from provincial dialects which occurred in the dialects of certain parts of England but which did not obtain a footing in the standard language. These forms are important since they offer a possible means of determining the regions in England from which came the colonists who set the speech patterns of the South. A number of words in the South represent in their origin merely dialectal forms of standard English. The language of eastern New England in the eighteenth century was similar to that of the South since both probably originated in the dialects of the southeast of England, but later the language of New England was influenced by the spelling book, the elocu-

tion book, and the school teachers of New England. There
is also evidence that New England consciously imitated British pronunciation. The desire to cultivate "correctness" of
speech may be interpreted as a mark of the cultural continuity between the New England and the Old, but it may also
be interpreted as a symptom of a feeling of inferiority which
the South did not have.

2. Brooks, Cleanth. The Relation of the Alabama-
Georgia Dialect to the Provincial Dialects of Great Britain.
(Louisiana State University Studies, No. 20.) Baton Rouge:
Louisiana State University Press, 1935. 91 pp.
　　　　Brooks says that provincialisms must have been transferred from Great Britain to America during the settlement
of America by British colonists. He raises two questions:
How many of these provincialisms have persisted? Is it possible to distinguish particular areas in Great Britain from
which the American dialects are derived? He concludes that
the Alabama-Georgia variants have their source in the dialects of the South of England and that many "negro" pronunciations in the southern counties of England may be considered the source of the change of initial th to d in American
Negro dialect since the change occurred early enough for
such variants to be brought over by the seventeenth-century
immigrants to America.

3. Cash, W. J. "Genesis of the Southern Cracker,"
American Mercury, XXXV (May, 1935), 105-108.
　　　　According to Cash, the source of the Southern Cracker
is the same as that of at least ninety per cent of all Southern
whites, but with the invention of the cotton gin and the spread
of the plantation to the back country, the poor-white was
driven back to the rejected lands and condemned to a life of
poverty. "The hunter who had formerly foraged for the
larder while his women hoed the corn now spent most of the
time on his back, disdaining to do work which habit had
fixed as effeminate, and consoling himself for the poorness
of the shooting with a jug of what he himself named 'bust-
head.'"

4. Greet, William Cabell. "Southern Speech," in
Culture in the South. Edited by W. T. Couch. Chapel
Hill: University of North Carolina Press, 1935, pp. 594-
615.
　　　　In addition to a discussion of Southern speech in general, Greet lists and explains thirty-three of the "most obvious" characteristics of the coastal and southern varieties

of speech. He also includes a short discussion of the speech of the southern hills.

5. McDavid, Raven I., Jr. "Dialectology: Where Linguistics Meets the People," The Emory University Quarterly, XXIII (Winter, 1967), 203-221.

McDavid gives a survey of the early approaches to linguistics by American scholars and an account of his own experiences and the skills he developed in his beginning field work with the Linguistic Atlas project. He mentions particularly his use of the phonetic alphabet in taking notes; his learning to work with informants of various races, social classes, and political opinions; his assessing the structure of a community from interviews with informants and with conversations with local inhabitants; his learning to make cultural appraisals through the menus of local restaurants, the kinds of churches in small towns as well as the presence or absence of saloons, and the conditions of country roads. From such knowledge, the field worker begins to look for signs that indicate the existence of dialect boundaries: the changing shapes of haystacks, the "set" of farmhouse chimneys, the patterns of residences, etc.

The dialectologist learns through his field experience to be data-oriented, not to reject the existence of a form because he has not encountered it, to record what people say and not what he thinks they intend to say, and to evaluate usage statements. McDavid suggests that Southern schools should develop more effective programs for teaching standard English in the schools. This can be done more easily in the South than in the North since in every Southern community the "educated and uneducated share the same system of phonemes, the same phonetic values and most of the same matters of phonemic incidence, and the grammatical characteristics of non-standard speech are shared by all races." The South is also the place where the teaching profession can most effectively begin its critical public relation task of explaining to the public "that educated speech can come in a variety of pronunciation patterns, and that every habitual variety of the language is acquired in the same way-- through contact with others who speak that variety."

6. McDavid, Raven I., Jr. "Go Slow in Ethnic Attribution: Geographic Mobility and Dialect Prejudices," in Varieties of Present-Day English. Edited by Richard W. Bailey and Jay L. Robinson. New York: Macmillan Company, 1973, pp. 258-270.

McDavid discusses the attitudes of speakers of different regional dialects and particularly the differences between
the speech of Southerners and that of other Americans.   He
says that there is no single variety of English that we can
call standard to the exclusion of other varieties.   "Leaving
aside the usage of other nations, the cultural facts are that
there is inherently nothing to place the usage of Massachusetts (eastern or western) above that of Minnesota, that of
New York above that of New Orleans, that of Texas above
that of Tennessee, that of Virginia above that of California. "
It is the speech to which one is accustomed that inspires the
favorable reaction.

McDavid says that one of the differences between the
speech of Southerners and that of other Americans is that of
range.   The pitch is both higher and lower than that of Midwestern speech and the stress is both stronger and weaker.
The prolongation of the stressed vowels gives the illusion of
drawl, although the tempo is faster than that of Midwestern.
The educated Southerner has a wider range between his spoken
and written language than does his counterpart in other regions.   Thus he may be accused of speaking carelessly.   In
pronunciation, there are relatively few differences between
cultivated Southern speech and that of other regions.   The
Southerner may simplify many consonant clusters and may
pronounce many vowel sounds differently from those used in
other sections.   Some grammatical features are considered
nonstandard English by those from other sections, but the
colloquial mode of educated Southern speech is similar to the
British speech of the colonial period, thus indicating that it
has lagged behind the rest of the English-speaking world.
The educated Southerner adapts his speech to the social occasion.   The uneducated will try to make the shift from informal to formal speech by using bigger words and longer
sentences, sometimes resulting in the ridiculous.   Few of
the uneducated know how to shift to the formal for the con-
ventions of writing.   Speech characteristics of the uneducated
in the South are not confined to the South.   They include uninflected plurals of nouns of measure; nouns ending in -sp,
-sk, and -s often have plurals in -iz; some differences in
the use of subject and object forms of personal pronouns;
some use of -n forms of absolute genitives; some tendency
to use inflected comparisons of adjectives and some use of
double comparisons.   Most of the nonstandard forms are
found in verbs.

7.   Mathews, M. M.   Some Sources of Southernisms.
University, Ala. : University of Alabama Press, 1948.   154
pp.

An enlarged version of three lectures concerned with Nahuatl, Muskhogean, and African words that have become part of the Southern vocabulary. An index of words from these three sources is included.

8. Norman, Arthur M. A. "A Southeast Texas Dialect Study," in Readings in American Dialectology. Edited by Harold B. Allen and Gary N. Underwood, N.Y.: Appleton-Century-Crofts, 1971, pp. 135-151. Reprinted from Orbis, V (1956-), 61-79.

A report of the investigation of the speech of Jefferson County, Texas, with attention to the speech of Chambers, Hardin, and Orange Counties, based on the writer's doctoral thesis at the University of Texas, 1955. Information on the settlements in the area came from the nativity tables for the Tenth Census of the settlement of the area in 1880. Worksheets for the study are based on Kurath's worksheets of 1939, revised 1949 by Davis and McDavid, and by Atwood in 1951. The informants were chosen to represent three age levels and three educational levels. Twelve informants were interviewed, nine from Jefferson County and one each from the other three counties.

A comparison of Kurath's key words for the North, the Midland, and the South, with the South Midland of Southwest Texas shows that Southern words are used twice as much as Midland expressions, which are used twice as much as Northern terms. It was also found that formally schooled informants change their vocabulary more rapidly than do the less educated and that they also prefer grammatically correct usage. The report also includes comparisons in vocabulary, in pronunciation, and in verb forms and syntactical peculiarities.

9. Walsh, Harry, and Victor L. Mote. "A Texas Dialect Feature: Origins and Distribution," American Speech, XLIX (Spring-Summer, 1974), 40-53.

The immigrants to Texas were mainly from the South, with their origin in the Middle Atlantic states. This study is concerned with the geographical distribution and the historical origins of the various treatments of a tauto-syllabic sequence consisting of a low-back or mid-back vowel followed by /r/ and one or more consonants, or VRC, in the Dallas-Fort Worth area, rural areas in and around Ellis County, including the towns of Waxahachie, Forreston, Italy, and Milford, Travis County, including the city of Austin and the greater Houston area of east Texas.

10. Wise, C. M. "Southern American Dialect,"
American Speech, VIII (April, 1933), 37-43.

Wise says that the typical speech is not that of the
most cultivated Southerner nor of the most ignorant, but of
a minority in a middle group. He makes the following gen-
eralizations about Southern dialect: the speech of educated
Southerners does not differ materially in vowel selection
from that in the general American area although there may
be a difference in the placement and quality of the vowels;
in the use of "r," Southern speech differs little from the
speech of Easterners or Britons; the "typical" Southern
speech may be produced by adding to educated Southern
speech a number of characteristics of less literate speech
if the intonation is Southern.

11. Wood, Gordon R. "Dialect Contours in the
Southern States," American Speech, XXXVIII (February-
December, 1963), 243-256. Reprinted in Readings in Amer-
ican Dialectology. Edited by Harold B. Allen and Gary N.
Underwood. New York: Appleton-Century-Crofts, 1971, pp.
122-134.

The purpose of this study is to show the regional vocabulary found in Alabama, Arkansas, Florida, Georgia,
Louisiana, Mississippi, Oklahoma, and Tennessee as determined by a postal questionnaire. The article is concerned
with the presence of Midland and Southern words in the areas
settled after 1800. Three phases of the region help to explain the diversity: the advancing frontier by way of the
Appalachian mountain valleys and gaps; the growth of towns
and permanent settlements; and the increase of regional communication.

12. Wood. Gordon R. Vocabulary Change. A Study
of Variations in Regional Words in Eight of the Southern
States. Carbondale and Edwardsville: Southern Illinois University Press, 1971. 392 pp.

An analysis of the responses of a thousand persons
born, reared, and living in Alabama, Arkansas, Florida,
Georgia, Louisiana, Mississippi, Oklahoma, and Tennessee,
to a printed vocabulary questionnaire. Chapter 1 traces the
patterns of settlements, urbanizations, and commerce. Chapter 2 discusses technical problems arising from the use of
the questionnaire to gather information and the use of com-
puters to count the responses. Chapter 3 considers the gross
word counts and examines them as clues to linguistic change.
Chapter 4 discusses the geography of selected regional words.
Chapter 5 provides a model of Southern dialect and its major

subdialects. Chapter 6 shows the relative importance of synonyms as they are reported in the eight states. Chapter 7 summarizes the material. Appendices give the ancestral origins of the informants, the questionnaire format, data processing notes, list of participating counties, occurrence of local words, totals of words used, volunteered list, and 84 word maps. Woods says that vocabulary shows the geographic limits of Southern dialect to extend from the South Atlantic states to the slopes of the Rockies, its northern boundary following the course of the Ohio to its joining with the Mississippi; then passing north of the Missouri Ozarks, it extends west along the northern boundary of Oklahoma.

Characteristics of Southern Speech

C. Alphonso Smith summarizes the characteristics of Southern dialect under seven general rules:[51] Like used for as if; 'low (allow) meaning think and say; such words as tune, news, duty (but not true, rule, sue, dude) have the vanishing y sound heard in few; the vanishing y sound is heard in gyarden, cyards, Cyarter, and the broad a is heard in Virginia; more, store, floor, four, and similar words are usually pronounced mo, sto, flo, fo by Negroes but given two distinct syllables by whites, the last syllable having the uh sound heard in mower; use of you all implying more than one person.

Raven I. McDavid, Jr., lists eleven features that are assumed to be characteristics of Southern speech, none of which, he says, is universal in the South, especially the drawl, for which "there is no evidence that Southerners on the average talk any more slowly than Midwesterners, and much evidence that some varieties of Southern speech-- notably that of the Charleston area in South Carolina--are much more rapid than the varieties of speech in the Middle West."[52] In addition to the drawl, McDavid includes you- all as a plural but allegedly as a singular; to tote, as groceries from the store; to carry a mule to the barn or a young lady to a party; the loss of post-vocalic /r/ in such words as barn, board; a so-called "Brooklyn diphthong" in bird and turn; the positional alternation of "fast" and "slow" variants of the diphthongs /ai/ and /au/; the appearance of monothongal [a.] for /ai/ before voiced consonants and finally, but not before voiceless, giving [a.] in ride but [ai] in write; the appearance of /ai/ as [a.] in all positions; the alleged falling together of /ai/ and /a/, so that blind and

blond become homonyms; the alleged falling together of /ai/
and /ae/ so that right is indistinguishable from rat.   McDavid
says that these "myths" persist because contrary evidence is
confined to scholarly articles.   Raymond D. Gastil says that
the Southern dialect uses diphthongs ("yes" becoming "ye-as";
"class" becoming "kla-yes"), and final consonants in consonant clusters may be dropped. 53

SOUTHERN LOWLANDER DIALECTS

Historical Background

The Lowland Southern includes the Virginia Tidewater,
which extends along the coast from the Delmarva (Delaware-
Maryland-Virginia) Peninsula to South Carolina; the South
Carolina Low Country, extending from the Peedee River, in
northeastern South Carolina to Northeastern Florida, with extensions along the river valleys as far inland as Columbia,
South Carolina, and Augusta and Macon, Georgia; and the
General Lowland type. [54]   The Lowland Southern omits the
'r' more generally than does Eastern New England.

Lowlander Dialects in Literature:
Early Period

Augustus Baldwin LONGSTREET (1790-1870) was born
in Augusta, Georgia.   He studied for two years at an academy in Willington, South Carolina, attended Yale for two
years, and studied law at Litchfield, Connecticut.   After re-
turning to Georgia, he served in the legislature, became a
judge of the superior court in Georgia, and in 1838 was or-
dained a minister.   He served as president of four colleges:
Emory; Centenary in Jackson, Louisiana; the University of
Mississippi; and the University of North Carolina.

Works:

"The Fight" and "The Horse-Swap, " in Georgia Scenes,
1835.   Sagamore Press.   Hill and Wang, and Peter Smith
have reprinted Georgia Scenes.

Richard Malcolm JOHNSTON (1822-1898) was born
near Powelton, Georgia, the son of a fox-hunting planter.
He graduated from Mercer College, and after a year of
teaching, became a lawyer.   From 1857 to the outbreak of
the Civil War he taught at the University of Georgia.   He

settled in Baltimore after the Civil War and began writing about life in Georgia in the thirties and forties. In the "Preface" to Mr. Absalom Billingslea and Other Georgia Folk, Johnston says: "As for the dialect, not only those who knew not better, but many of those who did, including some of the most eminent lawyers, were fond of it to the degree that they preferred it often, not only in sportive moods, but when incensed by resentment. It will be noticed that among most of the female characters in these sketches, even of the humbler sort, dialect is less pronounced than a-mong the men, thus proving its oft deliberate use and preference by the latter." Van Wyck Brooks calls attention to the fact that in one of the stories in Mr. Billingslea, Johnston took more than half a page to reproduce exactly the sound of a lisp. 55

Works:

Mr. Absalom Billingslea and Other Georgia Folk, 1887. Reprinted by Books for Libraries Press, 1970. 414 pp. Fourteen stories.

Dukesborough Tales. New York: D. Appleton and Company, 1871, 1874, 1883, 1892.

Primies and Their Neighbors; Ten Tales of Middle Georgia, 1891. Reprinted by Books for Libraries Press, 1969. 310 pp.

Little Ike Templin, and Other Stories, 1894. Reprinted by Books for Libraries Press, 1972. 259 pp. Thirteen stories.

Samuel Langhorne CLEMENS (1835-1910) was born in Florida, Missouri, a few months after his parents had moved from Tennessee. When Clemens was four, his family moved to Hannibal, on the Mississippi. While still a boy, he was apprenticed to a printer. Later he became a newspaper reporter and in 1857 began his apprenticeship to a Mississippi pilot. The Civil War brought his apprenticeship to a close and he went to Nevada with his brother and became a reporter for a newspaper in Virginia City. After two years he went to California and began to write humorous sketches for the Californian and the Golden Era. In 1867 he published his first book, a collection which included "The Celebrated Jumping Frog of Calaveras County." Huckleberry Finn was published in 1885.

Except for one scene the entire story of <u>Huckleberry Finn</u> is shown through the eyes of Huck, an uneducated boy, whose use of language, according to James M. Cox, transformed dialect into the vernacular, thus "making it the vehicle of vision. In terms of literary history, <u>Huckleberry Finn</u> marks the full emergence of an American language, and although Mark Twain did not accomplish the process alone, he <u>realized</u> the tradition which he inherited. "[56] Cox says that <u>instead</u> of imprisoning the dialect in a frame of literary language as other American humorists had done, Mark Twain allows Huck's vernacular to imply the literary form and thus reorganizes the entire value system of language, for all values had to be transmitted directly or indirectly through Huck's vernacular and the reader is forced to supply the implied norms. This inversion, Cox says, is the style of the novel. "And this style is Mark Twain's revolution in language, his rebellion in form; and it marks the emergence of the American language to which Hemingway and Faulkner allude when they say that Mark Twain was the first American writer, the writer from whom they descend. "[57]

J. Hillis Miller says that Huck's language is a "pungent vernacular" which thrives only outside society and is used by Mark Twain as an instrument for criticism of society. When Huck speaks as a member of society, he uses the false language of society which forces him to speak lies since the language of the community is the instrument of lies. When Huck and Jim are on the raft, his speech is honest and direct. When he is alone, Huck is at a loss for language, or he speaks the language of solitude, "a transformation of language from a means of communication into silence or into an inarticulate murmur, like the speech of elemental nature. "[58]

Works:

The Adventures of Tom Sawyer, 1876.

The Adventures of Huckleberry Finn, 1885.

Joel Chandler HARRIS (1848-1908) was born near Eatonton, Georgia. When he was thirteen he went to Joseph Addison Turner's plantation to set type for The Countryman. Here he listened to Negro stories in the cabins and gathered knowledge of both the Negroes and the rural whites. He also began to write short essays and poems which he inserted in the newspaper. After the war, he wandered from one newspaper office to another. He served on the staff of the Savannah Morning News and then joined the staff of the Atlanta Constitution, where from 1886 until his retirement in 1906 he held the position of chief editorial writer.

In 1880 the first of ten volumes of the Uncle Remus stories appeared. Other volumes include stories of other characters and scenes: Southern gentlemen, poor farmers, mountaineers, business men, and Negroes. Although Harris is best known for his Uncle Remus stories, his stories of the Georgia whites are important. "Better than any of his contemporaries except perhaps Mark Twain he could reproduce the speech of the rural whites. The Georgia dialect which his white characters speak is only a slightly archaic variety of the living 'American Language' of today."[59] Good examples of poor-whites in Harris's stories are Bud Stucky and his mother in "Azalia," in Free Joe, and Other Georgian Sketches, 1887.

Works:

Mingo and Other Sketches in Black and White, 1884.

Free Joe, and Other Georgian Sketches, 1887. Reprinted by Gregg Publishing Company, 1967.

Daddy Jake the Runaway, and Other Stories Told After Dark, 1889.

"The Kidnapping of President Lincoln," in On the Wing of Occasions, 1900. Reprinted by Books for Libraries Press, 1969, pp. 121-243.

Alice FRENCH (1850-1934) was born in Andover, Massachusetts, but spent the winters in the Black River country, Clover Bend, Arkansas. She wrote under the pen name of Octave Thanet.

Works:

A Captured Dream, 1897.

Stories That End Well, 1911.

"The Mortgage on Jeffy" and "The Loaf of Peace," in American Local-Color Stories. Edited, with an Introduction by Harry R. Warfel and G. Harrison Orions. New York: Cooper Square Publishers, Inc., 1970, pp. 484-513.

Lowlander Dialects in Literature:
Later Period

Frances GAITHER (1889-1955) was born in Somerville, Tennessee, but was brought up in Mississippi, where she attended Mississippi State College for Women. She married Rice Gaither, who worked for many years on the staff of the New York Times. Her stories have appeared in numerous magazines.

Works:

Follow the Drinking Gourd, 1940.

The Red Cock Crows. New York: Macmillan, 1944. 313 pp.

Double Muscadine. New York: Macmillan, 1949. 335 pp.

Marjorie Kinnan RAWLINGS (1896-1953) was born in Washington, D. C. She attended the University of Wisconsin, where she studied under William Ellery Leonard. In 1928, she went to live in Florida, in the Ocala Shrub, a jungle-like country bounded by the St. John's and Ochlawaha Rivers and lying within Marion County. She tells about her life among the Florida Crackers in Cross Creek, and she uses the dialect of the Cracker in many of her stories and novels.

William Joseph McGuire defines "Cracker" speech as "the speech of any of the early settlers of the Virginia and Carolina uplands--that is, most of the rural inhabitants of the mountains of West Virginia, Virginia, Kentucky, Carolina, Tennessee, Georgia; of the Ozark Mountains in Illinois, Missouri, and Arkansas; of the flatland backwoods of Georgia, Central and West Florida, Alabama, Mississippi, Louisiana, and east Texas."[60] W. J. Cash says that the invention of the cotton gin and the spread of the plantation to the back country pushed the small farmers back to the rejected lands-- the swamp and sand lands, the pine barrens and red hills-- where they were closed in and barred from any economic and social advance as a body.[61]

McGuire says that Mrs. Rawlings' handling of "central Florida dialect is, by and large, accurate and thorough despite her almost total lack of linguistic training or knowledge of the history of English. Her phonological notation is, necessarily, less adequate than her indication of morphology, syntax, and vocabulary. It should be emphasized that she treats the Cracker speech eclectically, which in view of her objective as an artist, is quite legitimate. "[62]

That Mrs. Rawlings had a sincere appreciation of the Cracker and his speech is shown in her characterizations and in her statement about the speech in "Jacob's Ladder": "The Cracker speech is soft as velvet, low as the rush of running branch water. "[63] She says that she took the tale of "A Plumb Clare Conscience" almost word for word from the oral account of a Cracker--a Carolinian by origin.[64]

Works:

South Moon Under. New York: Scribner's, 1933. 334 pp.

Golden Apples. New York: Scribner's, 1935.

The Yearling. New York: Scribner's, 1939. 428 pp.

When the Whippoorwill: Stories. New York: Scribner's, 1940.

Ben Lucien BURMAN (1895-   ) was born in Covington, Kentucky. He graduated from Harvard, became a journalist, ballad-writer, novelist, and writer of short stories. He is thoroughly acquainted with the mountain and river country that he writes about in his novels and stories. He has been a cub pilot on the Mississippi, a sailor, and even an amateur "hoodoo doctor" in order to get close to his Negro characters.

Works:

Mississippi. New York: Cosmopolitan Book Corporation, 1929.

Steamboat Round the Bend. Boston: Little, Brown and Company, 1933.

Blow for a Landing. New York: Houghton Mifflin Company, 1938.

Big River to Cross, 1940.

Everywhere I Roam, 1949.

Children of Noah, 1951.

William FAULKNER (1897-1962) was born in New Albany, Mississippi, but his family moved to Oxford, Mississippi when Faulkner was five years old. It is northern Mississippi that Faulkner uses for his literary territory-- Oxford as "Jefferson" and Lafayette County as "Yoknapatawpha County, " and it was here that he lived most of his life and where he wrote of the people and the life he knew.

Works:

Sartoris, novel. New York: Harcourt, Brace and Company, 1929.

Go Down, Moses: Stories. New York: Random House, 1942.

The Hamlet. New York: Random House, 1940.

As I Lay Dying. New York: Cape and Smith, 1930.

Caroline MILLER (1903-   ) was born in Waycross, Georgia, graduated from Waycross High School, and married her high school English teacher, William D. Miller. They were divorced and she later married Clyde H. Ray. They live in Waynesville, North Carolina.

Works:

Lamb in His Bosom, 1933, a novel of poineer life in the back country of Georgia in pre-Civil War days. It won the Pulitzer Prize for Literature in 1934.

Lebanon, 1944.

Robert Penn WARREN (1905-   ) was born in Guthrie, Kentucky but moved to Clarksville, Tennessee when he was eight years old. After his graduation from Vanderbilt University, where he was associated with John Crowe Ransom and Donald Davidson, he received an M. A. Degree at the University of California and spent a year at Yale. From

1928 to 1930 he was at Oxford on a Rhodes scholarship.   He
has taught at several colleges and universities.   In addition
to eleven books of poetry he has published ten novels, a collection of short stories, a biography, and numerous critical
articles.   He is also the co-author of several college textbooks.

Works:

Night Rider, novel.   Boston: Houghton Mifflin Company, 1939.   New York: Random House, 1948.

The Circus in the Attic and Other Stories; fourteen
stories including "Blackberry Winter."   New York: Harcourt,
Brace, 1947.

"Munn Short's Story," in World Enough and Time.
New York: Random House, 1950, pp. 419-425.

Caroline GORDON (1895-   ) was born at Merry
Mount Farm in Todd County, Kentucky.   She graduated from
Bethany College in West Virginia, taught school for a time,
and worked as a reporter on the Chattanooga News for four
years.   In 1924, she married Allen Tate, from whom she
was later divorced.   She has taught at Woman's College of
the University of North Carolina, at Columbia University,
and at the University of Dallas.   She was a Guggenheim Fel-
low in 1932.   She has written several novels and short
stories, and edited The House of Fiction, 1950, with Allen
Tate.

Works:

Penhally, novel.   New York: Scribner's, 1931.

Alex Maury, Sportsman, novel.   New York: Scribner's, 1934.

The Forest of the South, stories.   New York: Scribner's, 1945.

Old Red and Other Stories.   New York: Scribner's,
1963.   Cooper Square Publishers, 1971.   256 pp.   13 stories.

Eudora WELTY (1909-   ) was born in Jackson, Mississippi, where she now lives.   She attended the Mississippi

State College for Women and received the B. A. degree from the University of Wisconsin. After studying for one year in the School of Advertising at Columbia University, she returned to Jackson, where she worked at several jobs in journalism while beginning to write. In 1941 her first collection of short stories, A Curtain of Green and Other Stories, was published. "Why I Live at the P. O. " is in this collection. She has written several novels as well as another collection of stories. Robert W. Daniel calls her novel The Ponder Heart "a masterpiece of the comic imagination. " This term could also be applied to "Why I Live at the P. O. " The dialect in this story is characterized not so much by word choice and pronunciation as by arrangement of sentence parts and by its speech rhythms. The language is a key to the pathological state of the narrator and of the members of her family.

Works:

A Curtain of Green and Other Stories, with a critical preface by Katherine Anne Porter. Garden City, N. Y. : Doubleday, Doran, 1941.

The Ponder Heart, novel. New York: Harcourt, Brace, 1954.

Delta Wedding, novel. New York: Harcourt, Brace and Company, Inc. , 1946.

The Golden Apples, stories. New York: Harcourt, Brace and Company, Inc. , 1949.

The Optimist's Daughter, 1972.

Flannery O'CONNOR (1925-1964) was born in Savannah, Georgia. She received a B. A. degree from Georgia State College for Women in 1945, and an M. F. A. degree from the State University of Iowa in 1947. She was awarded a Kenyon Fellowship in Fiction, 1953-1954, the O. Henry Award in 1957, a grant from the National Institute of Arts and Letters, 1957, and a Ford Foundation grant in 1959-1960. She made her home in Milledgeville, Georgia.

Works:

A Good Man Is Hard to Find, and Other Stories. New York: Harcourt, Brace and Company, Inc. , 1953, 1954, 1955.

"Revelation," in Everything That Rises Must Converge. New York: Farrar, Straus and Giroux, 1964, 1965.

"... from a linguistic point of view, no language or dialect ... is inherently inferior to any other in its potential communicative efficiency. "

--William A. Stewart. "Language and Communication Problems in Southern Appalachia, " in Contemporary English. Change and Variation. Edited by David L. Shores. Philadelphia: J. B. Lippincott Company, 1972, p. 111.

SOUTHERN MOUNTAIN DIALECTS

Historical Background

The Southern mountain area--the Southern Appalachians and the Ozarks--includes the four western counties of Maryland, the Blue Ridge hills, the Allegheny Ridge country of Virginia, Eastern Kentucky, Eastern Tennessee, Western North Carolina, Northwestern South Carolina, Northern Georgia, and Northeastern Alabama, and the Ozark hills of Southern Missouri, Northwestern Arkansas, and the southeastern tip of Oklahoma, or a total of 142,000 square miles. [65] William A. Stewart says that Appalachia also includes all of West Virginia, as well as adjacent parts of Pennsylvania, Ohio, and Maryland. [66]

B. A. Botkin thinks that geographical isolation has been the dominant factor in the two mountain areas. He says that the Southern Appalachians were settled chiefly between 1800 and 1850 of Scotch-Irish and Germans from Pennsylvania, and English, Scotch, Irish, and French Huguenots from the Piedmont and Tidewater areas. After 1850, the migrations westward left the highland people isolated. They remained because they liked the simple life of living by hunting and fishing. [67]

Studies of the Mountaineer Dialects

1. Berrey, Lester V. "Southern Mountain Dialect," American Speech, XV (February, 1940), 45-54.
Berrey says that the dialect of the South Highlands should be distinguished from the illiterate usages of the lower mountains and other isolated districts. It is largely a survival of earlier English and is not a degradation of language. There are survivals of the literary language of Anglo-Saxon and Chaucer as well as pronunciation from the times of Shakespeare and Milton. In the Blue Ridge of West Virginia and in the Shenandoah Valley of Virginia there are remnants of the Scotch-Irish heritage. In the Ozarks near the

Oklahoma border, a few Indian terms are in common use.
Berrey discusses local differences in the dialect, pronunciation, consonant change, palatization, metathesis, parts of
speech, pleonasms, inverted compounds, portmanteau words,
and folk etymology. A bibliography on Southern mountain dialect is also included.

2. Campbell, John C. The Southern Highlander and
His Homeland. New York: Russell Sage Foundation, 1921.
405 pp.
    An account of the settlements, the people, their an-
cestry, their education, religion, economic opportunities,
etc., in the early years of the twentieth century. Five appendices provide additional data including historical estimates
of the Scotch-Irish and Germans in the United States in 1775.
A fourteen-page bibliography is included.

3. Chapman, Maristan. "American Speech as Practised in the Southern Highlands," Century, CXVII (March,
1929), 617-623.
    Chapman says that the speech of the Southern high-
lander is a genuine American dialect, for the highlanders
speak a cultured backwoods tongue all their own. The early
settlers were mainly Scotch-Irish who spoke the dialects of
their home counties. Others were Germans from the Rhine
Provinces or from colonies that had been settled in Pennsylvania and thus spoke Pennsylvania-Dutch. There were a few
Frenchmen and English immigrants from Suffolk who brought
a strain of Norman French. The isolation of the mountaineers allowed them to coin new words and their contact with
the Indians taught them other new words, but some words
and idioms were forgotten and others were dropped. The
pronunciation of some words is archaic and many old forms
of verbs are retained. There is confusion between strong
and weak verbs. The language is rich in having many shades
of words and in a feeling for the sounds of words.

4. Combs, Josiah. "Language of the Southern Highlander," PMLA, LXVI (1931), 1302-1322.
    Combs lists several pages of expressive usage, of
figurative language, of idiomatic language, of slang and "cuss
words," of coined words, of neologisms, of compounds, of
pleonasms, of nomenclature and pet names used in highland
speech. He also includes a discussion of syntax. He says
that there are three kinds of pronunciation in highland speech:
that of everyday speech, that employed in Baptist sermons,
and that employed in singing the folk-song.

5. Kephart, Horace. "The Mountain Dialect," in
Our Southern Highlanders. New York: Macmillan Company,
1949, pp. 350-378.
The hillsmen shorten words by elision but they insert
sounds where they do not belong--a consonant, a syllable, or
a word. Other characteristics are the substitutions of one
sound for another, mainly of vowels. The dialect varies
from place to place and sometimes even within a family.
Scotch influence appears in the pronunciation of r, which the
highlanders sound distinctly. The skipping of r is common
only where lowland influence has set in. The highlander
coins words wherever there is a need--by combination or by
turning nouns into verbs or otherwise interchanging the parts
of speech. Old English strong past tense lives in begun,
drunk, holped, rung, shrunk, sprung, stunk, sung, swum.
There are many corrupt forms of the verb. The syllabic
plural is preserved in such words as beasties, nesties,
posties, etc. Pleonasms are plentiful.

6. Miles, Emma Bell. "The Literature of a Wolf-
Race," in The Spirit of the Mountains. Knoxville, Tennessee:
The University of Tennessee Press, 1975, pp. 172-189. Fore
word by Roger D. Abrahams and Introduction by David E.
Whisnant. A Facsimile Edition of 1905 edition published by
J. Pott, New York.
Miles says that the speech of the mountaineers is a
genuine dialect and that many of the word forms are historic
and can only be found in literary works antedating the close
of the sixteenth century.

7. Randolph, Vance. "The Grammar of the Ozark
Dialect," American Speech, III (October, 1927), 1-11.
Randolph says that the chief differences between the
Ozark dialect and standard English are matters of pronunciation rather than of grammar. One of the most striking grammatical peculiarities of the Ozark speech is the use of weak
conjugation of the verb. Another is the use of was with the
second person singular, will for shall, and verbs fashioned
from nouns and adjectives. The hillman uses the objective
forms of the pronoun where the nominative form is needed,
the ending of n for the possessive instead of s, the plural
forms you-all and we-all. The pronoun does not always agree
with its antecedent in number; whose is not common and whom
is never used. Adverbs are replaced by adjectives. Double
negatives are common and even the triple and quadruple forms
are used. Adjectives are compared with er and est termina-
tions. Some Ozark nouns are converted verbs and a few sing-

ular nouns are used as if they were plural and some nouns serve as both singular and plural.

8. Reese, James Robert. "The Myth of the Southern Appalachian Dialect as a Mirror of the Mountaineer," in Voices from the Hills. Selected Readings of Southern Appalachia. Edited by Robert J. Higgs and Ambrose N. Manning. New York: Frederick Ungar Publishing Company, 1975, pp. 474-492.
Reese, who made a survey of American dialectology from 1889 to 1973 as a Ph.D. dissertation at the University of Tennessee, raises two questions in this essay. Is there a Southern Mountaineer dialect? In his attempt to explore the nature, mind, and culture of the Southern Mountaineer, what is a linguistically reasonable manner for the literary scholar to use in approaching the mountain speech?

9. Stewart, William A. "Language and Communication Problems in Southern Appalachia," in Contemporary English, Change and Variation. Edited by David L. Shores. Philadelphia: J. B. Lippincott, 1972, pp. 107-122.
Stewart calls the English used in Appalachia Mountain Speech, which he says is the linguistic legacy of the folk speech of the early settlers, many of whom came into the area from Pennsylvania, Maryland, Virginia, and the Carolinas during the latter part of the eighteenth century. Many Appalachians no longer accept Mountain Speech as respectable because of modern contacts with the outside and of in-migration, but the English of the educated natives is still Appalachian in sound. In addition to Mountain Speech, Negro Dialect is also present as a result of migration from the South Atlantic plantation area. It differs from the Mountain Speech of the rural whites and the city speech of the urban whites in many details of pronunciation, grammar, and vocabulary.

10. Williams, Cratis D. "Rhythms and Melody in Mountain Speech," Mountain Life and Work, XXXVII, 3 (Fall, 1961), 7-10.
Williams says that the rhythmic patterns of the speech of the Southern mountaineers are achieved by low intonations, leisurely pace, and the lack of self-consciousness in matters of grammar and diction. He lists characteristics of the speech--strong, past-tense forms of verbs, old-fashioned prepositions, pleonasms, contractions, archaic tags, etc. -- that produce a poetic folk quality. He mentions particularly the omission of g in ing endings, the indefinite article a,

the unstressed prefix be-, the syllable endings of certain
plural nouns and singular verbs in the third person of the
present tense, and certain adjectival inflections, all of which
give the speech of the mountaineer a melodic quality. Williams also lists certain forms used by the mountaineer as
being melodic: them for those, yourn for your one, ain't or
hain't for isn't, that instead of who and which. The mountaineer likes to use figures of speech, epigrams, superlative
phrases, and Biblical quotations.

11. Williams, Cratis D. "Verbs in Mountaineer
Speech," Mountain Life and Work, XXXVIII (Spring, 1962),
15-19.
According to Williams, the strength of the speech of
the mountaineer lies in the use of verbs and the economy
with which they function. Five verbs--begin, come, eat,
give, run--retain their infinitive forms throughout the tenses.
Such verbs as lay and set are used both transitively and intransitively. Other common verbs have the same form in
both past and perfect tenses. Were is normally used only
in the subjunctive constructions. Was is used for both singular and plural in the indicative mood. Strong verbs are
often weakened and irregular verbs made regular. The -d
and -ed endings of past forms of verbs are frequantly pronounced -t. Nouns and adjectives are often converted into
verbs. New verbs are sometimes coined.

12. Williams, Cratis D. "Who Are the Southern
Mountaineers?" in Voices from the Hills. Selected Readings
of Southern Appalachia. Edited by Robert J. Higgs and Ambrose N. Manning. New York: Frederick Ungar Publishing
Company, 1975, pp. 493-506.
Williams says that the Southern Highlands region begins with the Mason-Dixon Line on the north, follows east
of the Blue Ridge in a southwesterly direction into Georgia
just north of Atlanta, turns westward to Birmingham to include northwestern Alabama, and northward west of the Cumberland Plateau through Tennessee and Kentucky to the Ohio
River above Maysville, Kentucky. It returns along the Ohio
to the southwestern corner of Pennsylvania. It includes all
of West Virginia and spreads over parts of eight other states.
The highlander was part of the whole Westward Movement. He settled in the mountains because of the fertile land,
of good range for his cattle, and of the opportunity for hunting and fishing. Although there is a homogeneity of the eth-
ical and ethnic character of the mountain people, socially and
economically they fall into three groups: town and city dwel-

lers--nearly two million, of native stock, who resent being
called mountaineers; valley farmers--largest in number,
more less prosperous rural folk; branchwater mountaineers--
fewer in number than valley farmers, who live in coves, up
the branches, on the ridges, and are small holders of land
or are tenants.   The third type became the mountaineer of
fiction.

    13.   Wilson, Charles Morrow.   "Elizabethan America, "
Atlantic Monthly, CXLIV (July-December, 1929), 238-244.
    The speech of the Southern mountains is a survival of
the language of older days rather than a corruption of American English.   There is a preponderance of strong preterits,
plurals of monosyllables ending in -st by adding -es, the use
of words and pronunciations from Elizabethan times, the making of words and phrases to fit the occasion, the choice of
words determined by euphony and exactness of thinking.

Language of the Southern Mountaineers

    The language of the Southern mountaineer is a genu-
ine dialect and not a garbled version of standard usage.   "To
put into their mouths a stereotyped, manufactured dialect is
to rob them of their essential humanness and to present them
as comic stage-folk. "68   Claude M. Wise says: "Mountain
speech, taken in all its aspects, including the stylistic, has
a richness of quality not to be equaled in any other variety
of American speech. "69   Charles Morrow Wilson agrees:
"It is forceful speech.   It can clothe the most extraordinary
incident with matter-of-fact colors of reality and it can give
to casual bits of everyday life the most delicate shadings of
romance. "70

    Though fairly consistent, the dialect may vary with
the locality.   The four main divisions are the Blue Ridge of
Virginia and West Virginia, the Great Smokies of Tennessee
and North Carolina, the Cumberlands of Kentucky and Tennessee, and the Ozarks of Arkansas and southern Missouri.
Josiah Combs gives the general characteristics of the dialect. 71   The predominant elements, he says, are English,
with a touch here and there of Irish and Scottish.   Brevity
is preferred to clearness and grammatical accuracy.   The
speech is rich in idioms and expressive in figurative language.   It is also full of "cuss-words" or expressions of
surprise and intensity.   Words are coined when necessary
and old words are used with new meanings.   Pleonasm

is often employed for emphasis. The highlander is fond of pet names, diminutives, nicknames, and shortened forms.

In his discussion of the syntax of the dialect, Combs says that the singular is often used for the plural and the plurals of nouns are used excessively. The singular forms of the verb are used for plural forms, but the plural form for the singular is not common. Verbs are sometimes used as nouns and nouns as verbs. Transitive verbs are sometimes used intransitively. Lester V. Berrey says that contraction is the most common characteristic of mountain dialect, but almost as common is the dropping of partial pronunciation of a final letter. Intrusive sounds are also evident and there are frequent vowel and consonant changes. [72]

Southern Mountain Dialects in Literature: Early Period--Fiction

Sidney LANIER (1842-1881), a native of Macon, Georgia, gives in Tiger-Lilies one of the earliest serious treatments of the Southern mountaineer. Nathalie Wright says that "the native east Tennesseans in Tiger-Lilies speak and behave like true mountaineers. In fact, their speech, to which Lanier's ear was already attuned by the similar speech of the Georgia Crackers, is one of the earliest authoritative records of the language of southern Appalachia. Far more naturalistic than the caricaturing of his contemporary George Washington Harris, it equals in all but extent the later achievement of Mary Noailles Murfree."[73]

Works:

Tiger-Lilies, 1867. Reprinted with Introduction by Richard Harwell. Chapel Hill: University of North Carolina Press, 1969.

Katherine Sherwood BONNER (MacDowell) (1849-1883) was born in Holly Springs, Mississippi. In 1871 she married Edward MacDowell but separated from him two years later and went to Boston to earn her living. For a time she was secretary to Henry W. Longfellow, to whom she dedicated Like Unto Like, 1879, her first novel. In 1876 she went to Europe but returned in 1878 to Holly Springs to nurse her father and brother, both of whom died in the yel-

low-fever epidemic. She then devoted herself to writing
short stories, many in dialect, dealing with the Tennessee
mountains and with a section of Illinois that she knew. (Her
Gran'-mammy stories anticipated Russell in the use of Negro
dialect.)

Works:

Dialect Tales. Harper and Brothers, 1883. Reprinted by Books for Libraries Press, 1972. 187 pp. Eleven
stories.

Suwanee River Tales. Harper and Brothers, 1884.
Reprinted by Books for Libraries Press, 1972. 303 pp.
Includes six Gran'Mammy stories in Negro dialect.

Mary Noailles MURFREE (1850-1922) was born at
Grantland plantation near Murfreesboro, Tennessee. During
her early life she spent a few months each year visiting
Beersheba summer resort in the Cumberland mountains,
where she came in contact with the Tennessee mountaineers
that she portrays in her stories and novels. She is the
author of twenty-five published works, mainly fiction.

Works:

In the Tennessee Mountains. Eight stories, 1884.
Reprinted by The Gregg Press, Inc. , 1968; Tennessee Edi-
tion with an Introduction by Nathalie Wright. Knoxville,
Tennessee: University of Tennessee Press, 1970.

The Prophet of the Great Smoky Mountains, 1885.
Reprinted by AMS Press, 1970. 308 pp.

Will Nathaniel HARBEN (1858-1919) was born at Dal-
ton, Georgia. After a short and unsuccessful career as a
merchant in his home town, he moved to New York and made
a living by writing. He wrote twenty-seven novels, a collection of short stories, and two critical articles.

Works:

Northern Georgia Sketches, 1900. Ten stories that
had appeared in magazines. Reprinted by Books for Libraries Press, 1970. 305 pp.

John FOX, Jr. (1863-1919) was born in Paris, Kentucky. He attended Transylvania College for two years and then transferred to Harvard, graduating in 1883. He attended law school at Columbia University and went into the mining business at Big Stone Gap, Virginia.

Works:

Hell for Sartin' and Other Stories. New York: Harper and Brothers, 1897.

The Little Shepherd of Kingdom Come, 1903.

Christmas Eve on Lonesome, six stories. Scribner's, 1904. 234 pp.

The Happy Valley, stories. Scribner's, 1917.

Southern Mountaineer Dialects in Literature:
Early Period--Drama

Hatcher HUGHES (1893-1945) was born on a farm in the foothills of North Carolina. He graduated from the University of North Carolina in 1907 and became an instructor there in 1909. In 1911 he studied drama under Brander Matthews at Columbia University and became his assistant the next year.

Works:

Hell Bent fer Heaven, 1922. New York: Harper Brothers, 1924.

Lulu VOLLMER (1877-1955) was born in Keyser, North Carolina. She spent three years in the Normal and Collegiate Institute at Asheville, where she came in contact with mountain women who brought their wares to the Institute. While working as an accountant in the Piedmont Hotel in Atlanta, she wrote four plays and several short stories.

Works:

Sun-Up. New York: Brentano, 1923. Included in Arthur Hobson Quinn, Representative American Plays. Fifth Edition. New York: Century Company, 1930, pp. 982-1009.

The Shame Woman, 1923.

The Dunce Boy, 1925.

Trigger, 1927.

Paul GREEN (1894-   ) was born on a farm near Lillington, North Carolina. After graduating from Buie's Creek Academy, he entered the University of North Carolina but left to serve in World War I. He later resumed his studies at the University, studying under Frederich H. Koch and writing for the Carolina Playmakers. After graduation and a year of graduate work at Chapel Hill, he spent a year at Cornell and then returned to the University of North Carolina, later becoming Professor of Dramatic Art.

Green has written about the whites and the Negroes of the section he knew. (He had worked on his father's farm in close contact with both Negro and white workers.) Many of his plays are one-act plays. He also developed what he called "symphonic drama, " the use of various elements of the theater, mainly music and dancing, as part of folk drama. Many of his plays have been presented in out-door theaters.

Green was awarded the Pulitzer Prize for In Abraham's Bosom, 1926, the story of Abraham McCramie, a man half-white, half-black, trying to find his place in the world. In his review of the play, Stark Young says: "One of the best signs of promise in such a play as In Abraham's Bosom would lie in the ear; for nowhere in America is there better material for dialogue than in the world of Mr. Green's; no-where is there a more special rhythm and flavor or speech than in the South, or more warmth and naiveté of words than in Negro speech. "74 "Unto Such Glory" shows Green's knowl-edge of both the actions and the speech of the white people of rural North Carolina at the time of the play. Green also wrote stories and novels.

Works:

"Unto Such Glory, " in In the Valley and Other Caro-lina Plays. New York: Samuel French, 1928, pp. 145-171.

Out of the South. The Life of a People in Dramatic Form. New York: Harper and Brothers, 1939. 577 pp. Includes fifteen plays concerned with both Negroes and whites.

This Body the Earth, 1935. Novel of Southern share-croppers.

Salvation on a String, short stories, 1946.

Day on the Sun, a volume of short stories.   Chapel
Hill: University of North Carolina Press, 1949.   178 pp.

Southern Mountaineer Dialects in Literature:
Early Period--Poetry

Roy HELTON (1886-   ) was born in Washington,
D. C.   After graduating from the University of Pennsylvania
in 1908 and trying his hand at studying art and experiment-
ing with inventions, he became a school teacher.   Later he
spent some time in the mountains of South Carolina and Kentucky.

"Old Christmas Morning" is a ghost story told in
Kentucky mountain dialogue.   Old Christmas is the sixth day
of January, or the twelfth night after December 25.   Mildred
Haun has her narrator in The Hawk's Done Gone (p. 6) com-
ment of this date: "The cows all kneel at midnight on Old
Christmas to pray for any youngon born then.   They pray
that the youngon won'e ever die.   And it never will.   Or so
folks say.   The breath may go out sometime.   But the body
goes on doing the same thing it did while it was breathing.
Letitia Eades was born on Old Christmas.   That's the reas-
on she [the mountain] keeps on growing.   And will always. "

Works:

"Old Christmas Morning, " in Lonesome Water, 1930.

Stephen Vincent BENÉT (1898-1943) was born at Beth-
lehem, Pennsylvania, but spent his boyhood chiefly at army
posts, for his father was an army officer.   While a student
at Yale, he published a volume of poems.   After taking an
M. A. degree at Yale and a year at the Sorbonne, he settled
down to make a living by writing.   Before his death, he had
published about thirty volumes: novels, short stories, and
poems.

Works:

"The Mountain Whippoorwill, " in Selected Works of
Stephen Vincent Benét.   New York: Farrar and Rinehart,
Inc. , 1942, I, 376-380.

Southern Mountaineer Dialects in Literature:
Later Period

Olive Tilford DARGAN ("Fielding Burke") (1869-1968),
was born in Grayson County, Kentucky. When she was three,
her parents moved to Warm Springs, Arkansas, a resort in
the Ozark Mountains. In 1883, she entered Peabody Normal
College. After graduation, she taught in Southwest Missouri,
but went to Houston, Texas, to live with her aunt. For two
years she taught in San Antonio, Texas. She spent a year
in Cambridge, Massachusetts, where she took special work
in English at Radcliffe College. She then spent a year in
Canada and another year reading in the Boston libraries.
She had a physical break-down and went to live in northern
Georgia, where she met and married Pegram Dargan of
Darlington, South Carolina. Dargan has written dramas,
novels, and verse.

Works:

"Serena and the Wild Strawberries, " in Stories of the
South. Edited by Addison Hibbard. Chapel Hill: University
of North Carolina Press, 1931, pp. 169-193.

Call Home the Heart, 1932.

A Stone Came Rolling, 1935.

Lucy FURMAN (1870-1958) was born in Henderson,
Kentucky. After graduating from Sayre Female Institute in
Lexington, she took a secretarial course and went to work
in Evansville, Indiana, later becoming a court reporter.
She worked for a time with a Settlement School in the Kentucky mountains. She wrote of her experiences with the
small boys in Mothering on Perilous, 1913.

Works:

The Quare Women, 1923.

The Glass Window. Boston: Little, Brown and Company, 1925.

The Lonesome Road, a novel of mountain life, 1928.

Anne Wetzel ARMSTRONG (1872-1958) was born in Grand Rapids, Michigan. When she was quite young, her parents moved to Knoxville, Tennessee, a place that she used as a part of the setting for her first novel, The Seas of God, 1915. She attended Mt. Holyoke College and the University of Chicago. In the twenties, she went to live in the Big Creek Section of Sullivan County, Tennessee, where she wrote This Day and Time and where she lived until forced to move by the completion of the South Holston Dam. For an analysis of the dialect in this novel, see Earl F. Schrock, Jr., "An Examination of the Dialect in This Day and Time," in Voices from the Hills. Edited by Robert J. Higgs and Ambrose N. Manning. New York: Frederick Ungar Publishing Company, 1975, pp. 460-473. This essay is summarized on pages 25-26 of this book.

Works:

This Day and Time. New York: Alfred A. Knopf, 1930. Copyright 1953 by Roger A. Nayler. Reprinted by the Research Advisory Council, East Tennessee State University, Johnson City, Tennessee, 1970. 269 pp. This edition includes a personal reminiscence by David McClellan.

Edith Summers KELLEY (1884-1956) was born in Ontario, Canada. She graduated from the University of Toronto in 1903. She went to work in New York for Funk and Wagnall's Standard Dictionary. She was secretary to Upton Sinclair, 1906-1907. She became engaged to Sinclair Lewis but married Alan Updegraff, by whom she had two children. The marriage broke up and she lived with the sculptor C. Fred Kelley as his common law wife for fifty years.

Works:

Weeds. A novel of the tobacco fields of Kentucky. New York: Harcourt, Brace and Company, 1923, and London: Jonathan Cape, 1924. Reprinted by the Southern Illinois Press, with an Afterword by Matthew J. Bruccoli, 1972.

Elizabeth Madox ROBERTS (1886-1941) was born in Perryville, Kentucky, but grew up in the little town of Springfield, both towns on the edge of the Blue Grass region. This area was "then a quiet country of mixed farming and cattle-breeding, in sight of the Knobs, with the old ways of action,

thought, and speech to be found up any lane off the Louisville
pike, and sometimes on the pike.... In childhood, in young
ladyhood, and later as a lonely teacher in back-country
schools, Elizabeth Madox Roberts learned these old ways.
She knew the poetry of this pastoral quietness, but she knew,
too, the violence and suffering beneath the quietness. Her
stories grew out of the life of the place, and are told in a
language firmly rooted in the place. "[75]

The Time of Man, 1926, Roberts's first novel and the
novel that Ford Madox Ford says is the most beautiful novel
to come out of America, is the story of Ellen Chesser, the
daughter of a tenant farmer, and her wanderings all her "en-
duren life. " The language of the novel, says Robert Penn
Warren, "is an index of her [Ellen's] consciousness, and as
such is the primary exposition of her character and sensi-
bility. But it is also the language of her people, of her
place and class, with all the weight of history and experience
in it.... But it is not the color of the isolated turn that
counts most. It is, rather, the rhythm and tone of the whole;
and not merely in dialogue, but in the subtle way the language
of the outer world is absorbed into the shadowy paraphrase
of Ellen's awareness, and discreetly informs the general
style. "[76]

Donald Davidson says of The Time of Man: "What
most amazes me in this book is the dignity and naturalness
with which Miss Roberts uses the old colloquialisms of the
countryside, the brogue which has defeated so many inexpert
writers. Miss Roberts gets it down just as it ought to be.
The dialect of her characters is a triumphant example of
just what Southern country dialect really is, and seldom is
represented as being. But beyond that, dialect becomes in
her hands a real literary instrument. It is not a trick, a
superadded flavor of realism. You feel that it belongs in
the narrative. It is a kind of poetry in itself. "[77]

Works:

The Time of Man, 1926. New York: Viking Press,
1963. Compass Books Edition. Introduction by Robert Penn
Warren. Wood engravings by Clare Leighton. 397 pp.

My Heart and My Flesh. New York: Viking Press,
1927.

The Haunted Mirror, stories. New York: Viking
Press, 1932.

Black Is My Truelove's Hair.   New York: Viking Press, 1938.

Not by Strange Gods, stories.   New York: Viking Press, 1941.

Thames Ross WILLIAMSON (1894-   ) was born on the Nez Percé Indian Reservation near Genesee, Idaho.   He graduated from the University of Iowa in 1917 and received the M. A. degree from Harvard in 1918.   From 1920 to 1921 he taught economics at Smith College.   He has written thirteen novels as well as textbooks and books for children. Williamson believes that dialect should serve the purposes of the novelist and should not be used merely for its own sake. "It must bend to the superior hand, and change its form as words change stress and pronunciation when instead of speaking them, as ordinarily you sing them. "78

Works:

The Woods Colt, a Novel of the Ozark Hills.   Illustrated by Raymond Bishop.   New York: Harcourt, Brace and World, Inc. , 1933.   288 pp.

Emmett GOWEN (1902-   ) was born in Nashville, Tennessee.   He attended Columbia University and now lives at Lavergne, Tennessee.   He has contributed stories and articles to Scribner's, Story, Yale Review, and Atlantic.

Works:

"Hill Idyl, " short novel, Scribner's, XCII (July-December, 1932), 338-343, 375-384.

"Fiddlers on the Mountain, " in Today's Literature. Edited by Dudley Chadwick Gordon, Vernon Rupert King, and William Whittingham Lyman.   New York: American Book Company, 1935, pp. 104-114.

Mountain Born.   Indianapolis: Bobbs-Merrill Company, 1932.

Dark Moon of March.   Indianapolis: Bobbs-Merrill Company, 1933.

Old Hell.   Modern Age, 1937.

Maristan CHAPMAN is the pen name used by John Stanton Higham Chapman and his wife, Mary Hamilton Illsley Chapman. She was born in 1895 at Chattanooga, Tennessee. He was born in London, England, in 1891. They have been co-authors of several books and have written mystery stories under the name of "Jane Selkirk." Their short stories have appeared in The Atlantic, Century, and the Saturday Evening Post.

Works:

"Sib to We'Uns," Century, CXVII (November, 1928), 20-25.

"Treat You Clever," in O. Henry Prize Stories of 1929. Selected and edited by Blanche Colton Williams. New York: Doubleday, Doran and Company, 1930, pp. 143-161. Appeared originally in Saturday Evening Post, March 30, 1929.

"Crowded," in Golden Tales of the Old South. Selected and with an Introduction by May Lamberton Becker. New York: Dodd, Mead and Company, 1930.

The Happy Mountain, novel. New York: The Viking Press, 1928. 313 pp. Three pages of "Glossary."

Homeplace, novel. New York: The Viking Press, 1929. 275 pp. Three pages of "Glossary."

The Weather Tree, novel. New York: The Viking Press, 1932.

Thomas WOLFE (1900-1938) was born in Asheville, North Carolina. After graduating from the University of North Carolina, he spent two years at Harvard studying the writing of drama in George Pierce Baker's "47 Workshop." Between 1924 and 1938 he taught at New York University, traveled abroad, and began to write fiction. Floyd C. Watkins calls the story "Chickamauga" "one of the most effective representations of mountaineer speech in American literature."[79] Wolfe says that he got the idea for the story from his great-uncle, John Westall.[80]

Works:

From Death to Morning, stories. New York: Charles Scribner's Sons, 1935; reissued in 1958.

The Hills Beyond, stories. New York: Harper and Brothers, 1941. Includes "Chickamauga, " first published in The Yale Review, Winter, 1938.

Vance RANDOLPH (1892-   ) is a native of Pittsburg, Kansas. He graduated with a bachelor of science degree from the State Teachers College at Pittsburg and with a master's degree in psychology from the University of Worcester. He became a graduate assistant in biology at the University of Kansas and began work on a doctoral degree but left to return to the Ozarks.

Works:

Who Blew Up the Church House? And Other Ozark Folk Tales. New York: Columbia University Press. Illustrations by Glen Rounds with Notes by Herbert Halpert, 1952. 232 pp.

Down in the Holler: A Gallery of Ozark Folk Speech (with George P. Wilson). Norman, Okla.: University of Oklahoma Press, 1953.

James STILL (1900-   ) was born at Double Creek in Alabama. He attended Lincoln Memorial University and received an M. A. degree from Vanderbilt University. He also received a degree in library science from the University of Illinois. He was librarian at the Hindman Settlement School, Knott County, Kentucky, for several years. He lives at Wolfpen Creek, near Mallie, Kentucky. Hounds on the Mountain, his first volume of poetry, was published in 1937. He draws upon his own experience and knowledge of mountain people in his stories.

Works:

"So Large a Thing as Seven, " in O. Henry Memorial Award Prize Stories of 1938. Selected and edited by Harry Hansen. New York: Doubleday, Doran and Company, Inc., 1938, pp. 267-276. Reprinted from The Virginia Quarterly Review, 1937.

On Troublesome Creek, stories. New York: The Viking Press, 1940.

River of Earth, novel. New York: The Viking Press, 1940.

"The Proud Walkers," in O. Henry Memorial Award Prize Stories of 1941. Selected and edited by Herschel Brickell. New York: The Book League of America, pp. 289-304.

"The Egg Tree," in The Yale Review Anthology. Edited with an Introduction by Wilbur Cross and Helen MacAfee. Freeport, N. Y.: Books for Libraries Press, 1942, 1970. Reprinted 1971, pp. 354-363.

"A Master Time," Atlantic Monthly, CLXXXIII (1949), 43-46. Reprinted in Voices from the Hills, Selected Readings of Southern Appalachia. Edited by Robert J. Higgs and Ambrose N. Manning. New York: Frederick Ungar Publishing Company, 1975, pp. 253-262.

"The Burning of the Waters," Atlantic Monthly, CLXXXXVIII (October, 1956), 55-60.

Jesse STUART (1907-   ) lives in W-Hollow, about five miles from Riverton, Kentucky, in the same valley in which he was born. He graduated from Lincoln Memorial University and attended Peabody College and Vanderbilt University. He has taught school, served as superintendent of schools, lectured, farmed, and written numerous volumes of poetry, fiction, and nonfiction. He has received many rewards for his literary work including a Guggenheim Fellowship for travel in Europe, 1937, and the Thomas Jefferson Southern Award for his novel, Taps for Private Tussie, 1943.

Works:

Head O' W-Hollow, 21 stories, 1936. Reprinted by Books for Libraries Press, 1971. 342 pp.

Trees of Heaven, novel. Decorations by Woodi Ishmael. New York: E. P. Dutton, 1940, 340 pp.

Beulah Roberts CHILDERS (1906-   ) is a native of Berea, Kentucky. After graduating from Berea College, she

received an M. A. degree from Columbia University. She
has taught at Purdue and at the University of Oregon.

Works:

   "Sairy and the Young'uns, " in A Southern Harvest,
Short Stories by Southern Writers. Edited by Robert Penn
Warren. Boston: Houghton Mifflin Company, 1937, pp. 195-
211.

   Charles Garland GIVENS (1899-1964) was born in Dayton, Tennessee. He became a newspaperman and worked for
the Detroit Free Press, The Times Picayune in New Orleans,
and The Herald Examiner in Chicago. He wrote many stories
and several novels, three of which deal with life in East Tennessee.

Works:

   All Cats Are Gray.   Indianapolis: Bobbs-Merrill,
1937. 359 pp.

   The Doctor's Pills Are Star Dust. Indianapolis:
Bobbs-Merrill, 1938. 314 pp.

   The Devil Takes a Hill Town. Indianapolis: Bobbs-
Merrill, 1939. 396 pp. (Adapted into a Broadway play in
1948.)

   James AGEE (1909-1955) was born in Knoxville, Tennessee. He graduated from Harvard in 1932. In addition
to two novels, he wrote a volume of poems; a book of social criticism, Let Us Now Praise Famous Men, with photographs by Walker Evans, 1941; and numerous scripts including the film script for The African Queen.

Works:

   The Morning Watch, short novel. New York: Houghton Mifflin, 1951.

   A Death in the Family, written 1955. New York:
McDowell, Obolensky, 1959. 339 pp. Dramatized by Tad
Mosel under the title All the Way Home, 1960.

The Collected Stories of James Agee.   Edited and
with a Memoir by Robert Fitzgerald.   Boston: Houghton
Mifflin Company, 1968.

Mildred HAUN (1911-1966) grew up in Cocke County,
Tennessee, at the head of Haun Holler, Hoot Owl District. 81
She attended high school in Franklin, Tennessee, and then
went to Vanderbilt University, where in her senior year she
enrolled in John Crowe Ransom's course in Advanced Composition.   In this class she began to write stories of her
East Tennessee background.   When Ransom left Vanderbilt
in 1937, he turned her writing over to Donald Davidson,
under whose direction she had collected and edited Cocke
County Ballads and Songs as an M. A. thesis.   After a second post-graduate year at Vanderbilt and a writing fellowship
at the University of Iowa, her book of stories was published
in 1940 as The Hawk's Done Gone.
Herschel Gower says of this book: "No other dialect
collection from the South has been as close to the oral tradition or has achieved the same distinctive flavor and natural
tonal qualities" (p. xv).   He comments on the speech of one
of the chief narrators, the Granny-woman, Mary Dorthula
White: "Her speech strikes the ear directly from the printed page.   The language we hear carries with it the thrust
of simplicity and raw strength.   The words are coarse,
flinty, and staccato fragments.   In these unseasoned materials of literature there is no place for circumlocution, none
for convoluted rhetoric and tortuous syntax.   The meaning
lies not in memorable phrases, but, as in the ballads and
other oral forms, in the effects achieved with a sparse, direct economy" (p. xviii).   He notices that the diction characterizes the "rationale and temper of the narrator, " and
that "the figures of speech are taken directly from likenesses
in the natural world. "

Works:

The Hawk's Done Gone and Other Stories.   Nashville,
Tennessee: Vanderbilt University Press, 1968.   Introduction
by Herschel Gower.   Copyright by Mildred Haun, 1940.   356
pp.

Marie CAMPBELL is a native of Alexander County,
Illinois, but lived for some time with the Laurel Mountain
people of Kentucky.   She received the M. A. degree from

Peabody College in 1937 and the Ph. D. degree from Indiana
University in 1956. She was awarded a Guggenheim Fellowship in Creative Writing, 1944-1945.

    Alice V. Keliher says of Cloud-Walking: "I have
read books by authors using dialect before this, but that is
just what they had done--they had 'used' dialect to give local
color. But here is something far different. Here the writer
thinks with the words these people use in thinking, and my
deep impression is that I know these people immediately because I have heard them speak from their own minds."[82]

    Works:

    Cloud-Walking, with a foreword by Alice V. Keliher.
Illustrated by J. A. Spelman, III. New York: Farrar and
Rinehart, Inc., 1942. 272 pp.

    Harriette F. ARNOW (1908-   ) was born in Wayne
County, Kentucky. She attended Berea College and received
her bachelor's degree from the University of Louisville.
She lives with her husband, Harold B. Arnow, in Ann Arbor,
Michigan. In addition to novels, she has written two books
on the history of the old Southwest.

    Works:

    Hunter's Horn. New York: Macmillan Company,
1949. 508 pp.

    The Dollmaker. New York: Macmillan Company,
1954. 549 pp.

    The Weedkiller's Daughter. New York: Alfred A.
Knopf, 1970. 371 pp.

NEGRO DIALECT

Studies of Negro Dialect

1. Anshen, Frank. "Some Statistical Bases for the Existence of Black English," The Florida FL Reporter, X, Nos. 1 and 2 (Spring/Fall, 1972), 19-20.

Anshen presents and answers three major arguments used by those who deny the existence of Black English: the idea of Raven I. McDavid, Jr., that it is nonsense to say that black and white speakers can be identified by their speech; the statement of Hans Kurath that the speech of uneducated Negroes differs little from that of illiterate whites; and the argument of Juanita Williamson that features of Black English also occur in the speech of whites and that relative frequency of occurrence is irrelevant to linguistic analysis. Anshen obtains the data for refuting these arguments by considering the distribution among white and black groups in Hillsborough, North Carolina, of two phonological traits: the deletion of phonetic realization of /r/ in non-prevocalic position and the replacement of /ng/ by /n. in present participles. The data presented in six tables show that the variation in pronunciation associated with race is of greater magnitude than variation in pronunciation associated with education, sex, or age when considered within racial groups. "Not only are there clear differences between black and white speech in Hillsborough, but race is the most important single determiner in a person's speech."

2. Baratz, James C. "'Ain't' Ain't No Error," The Florida FL Reporter, IX, Nos. 1 and 2 (Spring/Fall, 1971), 39-40, 54.

Baratz says that the features of black nonstandard English form a unique system. A few of the features are as follows: ain't used for negation especially with predicate adjectives; use of zero copula more widespread in black nonstandard than in white nonstandard; use of zero copula and uninflected be to indicate continued action; the use of uninflected third person singular of regular verbs and inversion of the verb to express the standard if + clause construction;

87

failure to use inflection to mark the possessive. The training of most English teachers, says Baratz, does not allow
the teachers to conceive of a nonstandard dialect as a legitimate language, but learning standard English means adding
knowledge of another dialect for use in those situations where
it is appropriate. It does not mean eliminating black nonstandard English. Rejection of the idea that a different linguistic system exists by both blacks and whites leads to further difficulties in race relations.

3. Black English, A Seminar. Edited by Deborah
Sears Harrison and Tom Trabasso. Hillsdale, N. J.: Lawrence Erlbaum Associates, Publishers, 1976. 301 pp.
Papers presented at a seminar at Princeton University during the fall semester of 1973. The sixteen chapters
are divided into four groups, each group focusing on a different aspect of Black English: on its definition, on its historical origins, on its usage, and on its implications.

4. Brewer, John M. "Ghetto Children Know What
They're Talking About, " The New York Times Magazine, December 25, 1966, pp. 33-37.
The private speech of the children of the ghettos of
America is colorful and subtle, a language little known to
the outside world. It is developed by children even before
they come to school and is passed on from mother to child,
but is not used in front of outsiders. As children advance
in school, they also advance their hidden language. Brewer
tells how he helped the children to realize the disadvantage
of their idiomatic phrases by having them provide synonyms
for their well-known idioms by using the dictionary, by reading books, and by using other conventional means of winning
the "capping" game.

5. Burling, Robbins. "Black English, " in Man's
Many Voices, Language in Its Cultural Context. New York:
Holt, Rinehart and Winston, Inc. , 1970, pp. 117-133.
Burling says that it is the experience of the speaker,
particularly his early childhood experience, that determines
how he speaks, not his race. Although the English of many
Negroes shows characteristics of the southern United States,
not all of the linguistic features are found in either southern
or northern white dialects. This difference may indicate
that the unique character of Black English derives from a
history separate from that of white English. It may even
show the influence of the time when slaves were first im-
ported into this country or a trace of their African origin.

Although there are differences in standard middle-class English and the speech of some urban Negroes--phonological, grammatical, lexical, and semantic--many Negroes are able to shift from one extreme to the other, but the language of many Negro children of the northern ghettos is so different from that of standard English as to present educational and economic problems. One answer, Burling thinks, is to encourage bidialectism and to persuade teachers of Negroes that the native Negro dialects are of value to their users and deserve both understanding and respect.

6. Dillard, J. L. Black English, Its History and Usage in the United States. New York: Random House, 1972. 361 pp.

An investigation into the ways Black English differs from other varieties of American English. Dillard thinks that the differences may be traced to historical factors such as the language contacts connected with the West African slave trade and to survivals from West African languages. The seven chapters are concerned with Black English and the academic establishment, the structure and history of Black English, pidgin English in the United States, Negro dialect and Southern dialect, the speakers of Black English, and Black English and Education. Also included are a glossary of linguistic terms, an appendix "On the Pronunciation of Black English," and a bibliography of studies of Black English.

7. Fasold, Ralph W. "Distinctive Linguistic Characteristics of Black English," in Report of the Twentieth Annual Round Table on Linguistics and Language Studies. Edited by James E. Alatis. Washington, D.C.: Georgetown University Press, 1970, pp. 233-238.

Although research may reveal that there are some features of Black English that are different from anything in any English dialect spoken by whites, most of the differences are relatively superficial. However, the differences are stigmatized socially, and can contribute to the limitation of opportunity for those who speak Black English. Attempts to eradicate these features may be harmful to the child's self-esteem. These speech forms also follow rigorous rules of their own.

8. Fasold. Ralph W., and Walter A. Wolfram. "Some Linguistic Features of Negro Dialect," in Contemporary English. Edited by David L. Shores. Philadelphia: J. B. Lippincott Company, 1972, pp. 53-85. Reprinted from

Teaching Standard English in the Inner City. Edited by Ralph W. Fasold and Roger W. Shuy. Washington, D. C.: Center for Applied Linguistics, 1970, pp. 41-86.

Fasold and Wolfram preface their discussion by making three statements about Negro dialect: not all Negroes speak Negro dialect; Negro dialect shares many features with other kinds of English; Negro dialect is a "cohesive linguistic system" substantially different from standard American English dialects. The features of Negro dialect discussed in detail are pronunciation (word-final consonant clusters, the th- sounds, r and l, final b, d, and g, nasalization, vowel glides, indefinite articles a and an, stress, etc.) and grammar (verbs, negation, -s suffixes, questions, pronouns, pronomial apposition, existential it). The authors call attention to their use of rules based on actual usage rather than on rules in the traditional sense. "Negro dialect and other nonstandard linguistic systems operate under rules just as do socially favored dialects. But the rules are different."

9. Harrison, J. A. "Negro English," in Perspectives of Black English. Edited by J. L. Dillard. The Hague: Mouton and Company, 1975, pp. 143-195. Reprinted from Anglia, 1884.

An outline of Negro language usage in the South with numerous examples of the language selected from reputable writers such as J. C. Harris and Sherwood Bonner.

10. Haskins, Jim, and Hugh F. Butto. "The Genesis of Black American Dialects," in The Psychology of Black Language. New York: Barnes and Noble Books, 1973, pp. 28-37.

Haskins and Butto say that all blacks can trace their heritage to some part of Africa and that there are as many different kinds of blacks as there have been environmental determinants to affect them.

11. Labov, William. Language in the Inner City. Studies in the Black English Vernacular. Philadelphia: University of Pennsylvania Press, 1972. 412 pp.

Labov uses "black English vernacular" to refer to the speech of black youth from eight to nineteen years of age who are part of the street culture of the inner cities. The major concern of the study is to determine the relation between the reading failure in the New York City schools and the dialect of the students. The material is the work of four investigators: Labov, Paul Cohen, Clarence Robins, and John Lewis. The book is divided into three parts:

Part I, chapters 1-4, deals with the grammar and sound system of black English vernacular. Part II, chapters 5-7, is concerned with the vernacular in its social setting, the relations between the social system and the vernacular culture. Part III, chapters 8-9, is concerned with the uses of black English vernacular: "Rules for Ritual Insults," and "The Transformation of Experience in Narrative Syntax." The chief conclusion of the study is that the major problem in reading failure is the political and cultural conflict within the classroom.

    12.   McDavid, Raven I., Jr., and Virginia Glenn McDavid. "The Relationship of the Speech of American Negroes to the Speech of Whites," American Speech, XXVI (February, 1951), 3-17.
    Any scholar studying American Negro speech must discard the widely-held idea that Negro speech can be identified solely on the basis of Negro physical characteristics and he must show that some speech forms of Negroes may be derived from an African cultural background by the normal process of cultural transmission. The relationship between Negro and white speech must be evaluated in the same scientific spirit as an anthropologist studies acculturation. Ethnocentric prejudice of all kinds must be discarded and conclusions must be based on valid data. The following framework for arriving at conclusions is suggested: the bulk of American Negro speech is borrowed from the speech of white groups with which the Negroes came in contact and many relic forms from English dialects are better preserved in the speech of some American Negro groups than in white speech because of their isolation; the whites have also borrowed speech forms from the Negroes such as for for a particle with the infinitive of purpose; the Negro playmates of well-to-do white children and the Negro servants are partially responsible for the higher degree of tolerance of nonstandard forms in cultured speech in the South than elsewhere; the tendency in Southern speech to simplify final consonant clusters is encouraged by the Gullah and African languages; the intonation patterns in such communities as Charleston and Georgetown suggest Negro influence. Future work should include the study of Americo-Liberian English and old Negro communities outside of the South; there should be an early survey of Newfoundland and an intensive study of selected communities in the Maritime Provinces and of the Bank Islands on the North Carolina coast; Negro informants should be selected from several age and educational groups and in terms of the number of generations the families of informants have been residents in the community.

13. Mitchell, Henry H. "Black English," in Language, Communication, and Rhetoric in Black America. Edited by Arthur L. Smith. New York: Harper and Row, 1972, pp. 87-110. Reprinted from Black Preaching. Philadelphia: J. B. Lippincott, 1970.

Mitchell says that the features that distinguish Black English from Standard English include a slower rate of delivery, simpler sentence structure, a drawl, failure of agreement between subjects and verbs, and different use of function words. He attributes the differences in language to Black experience which is different from that of whites in the same area.

14. Morse, J. Mitchell. "The Shuffling Speech of Slavery: Black English," in The Irrelevant English Teacher. Philadelphia: Temple University Press, 1972, pp. 81-95.

Morse thinks that since Standard English is the English in which most of the books, magazines, and newspapers are written, the ability to read, write and speak it is a necessary key to the information and artistry found in books and as a way of avoiding linguistic maladjustment in communities that use Standard English. Standard English is also a medium for communication of precise information and for the development of clear ideas. "Localisms, regionalisms, and classisms should be avoided if they impede thought or study. A person whose habitual way of expressing such agreement differs from the standard way must suffer a disadvantage when he comes to read a book."

15. Perspectives on Black English. Edited by J. L. Dillard. The Hague: Mouton and Company, 1975. 391 pp.

A collection of essays on Black English organized under four heads with a general introduction of twenty-four pages by Dillard. The first section on the theory and method of Black English Dialectology includes five essays; the second section on the history of Black English includes eleven essays with an appendix; the third section, concerned with Black English and the acculturation process, has three essays; the fourth section of four essays is concerned with Black English and psycholinguistics.

16. Smith, Riley B. "Research Perspectives on American Black English: A Brief Historical Sketch," American Speech, XLIX (Spring-Summer, 1974), 25-39.

A survey of the studies of and attitudes toward American Black English from 1884 to the present. Smith concludes that since research in Black English has thus far been "data-poor," it is important not only to develop new techniques of research and description for studying urban speech where the problem of dialect differences is not obvious, but data should also be gathered in the area from which the initial outward migrations began and which gave rise to the urban puzzle, that is, of the rural South. A list of references of the study of Black English is included.

17. Stewart, William A. "Continuity and Change in American Negro Dialects," in Readings in American Dialectology. Edited by Harold B. Allen and Gary N. Underwood. New York: Appleton-Century-Crofts, 1971, pp. 454-467. Reprinted from The Florida FL Reporter, 6, No. 1 (Spring, 1968), 3-4, 14-16, 18. Also in Perspectives on Black English, pp. 233-247.

Stewart says that many of the Negro slaves spoke a variety of English which differed in grammatical structure from the English dialects brought directly from Great Britain, and that the non-standard speech of present-day American Negroes may be explained by this creole predecessor. He says that a comparison of Negro dialect of the period of the Civil War and that of today reveals both continuity and change in the dialect. One of the changes is the almost complete decreolization of both the functional and lexical vocabulary. There is evidence that some of the particular syntactic features of American Negro dialects are structural vestiges of an earlier plantation creole, and ultimately of the original slave-trade pidgin English which gave rise to it. Stewart says that such evidence calls for a complete reassessment of the relationships between British and American dialects and the pidgin and creole English of Africa and the Caribbean.

18. Stewart, William A. "Historical and Structural Bases for the Recognition of Negro Dialect," in Report of the Twentieth Annual Round Table on Linguistics and Language Studies. Edited by James E. Alatis. Washington, D. C.: Georgetown University Press, 1970, pp. 239-247.

Linguists should look to non-European sources for the features of Negro speech that are different from those of whites and should re-evaluate early literary records of American Negro speech as a basis of settling disputed or unclear points about the processes by which Negro dialect forms have come about.

19. Stewart, William A. "Observations (1966) on the Problems of Defining Negro Dialect," Postscript 1971, in The

Florida FL Reporter, IX, Nos. 1 and 2 (Spring/Fall, 1971), 47-49, 57.

In these observations, Stewart attempts to answer the question: "What is the linguistic behavior of uneducated Negroes like, and how does it compare with that of educated Negroes and of both uneducated and educated whites?"

20. Stewart, William A. "Understanding Black Language," in Black America. Edited by John F. Szwed. New York and London: Basic Books, Inc., Publishers, 1970, pp. 121-131.

In no part of the United States do Negroes and whites speak identically. This is especially true of Negroes of a low socio-economic class and of both whites and Negroes who haven't been strongly influenced by education. The slave owner justified slavery by claiming intellectual inferiority of the Negro which necessitated white caretakership. The distinct characteristics of Negro dialect became tied up with the idea that the Negro was innately inferior. Research in social group differences in language is being used by the scholar, and children are now being taught to read in terms of their own language patterns. It has been found that if the sentence structure is changed to match the sentence structure of the child, it is not necessary to change the spelling. Stewart says that standard English speakers will become more tolerant of language differences when they know something about the origins, structure, and vitality of various kinds of English, knowledge that will contribute to interracial harmony in the United States.

21. Williamson, Juanita Virginia. A Phonological and Morphological Study of the Speech of the Negro of Memphis, Tennessee. PADS, Number 50, November, 1968. 54 pp.

A revision of a Ph. D. dissertation, University of Michigan, 1961, designed to describe certain of the phonological and morphological features of the speech of the Negro of Memphis, Tennessee. The study is limited to a description of the segmental phonemes, their occurrence in the speech of both the educated and those with little education, and to a description of selected features of the forms of the noun, the pronoun, and the verb. The short work sheets of the Linguistic Atlas of the United States and Canada were used with some changes. Twenty-four informants, ranging in age from twenty-seven to eighty-four years, were interviewed for the study. All except one were natives of Memphis.

22. Wise, C. M. "Negro Dialect," in Perspectives on Black English. Edited by J. L. Dillard. The Hague: Mouton and Company, 1975, pp. 216-221. Reprinted from Quarterly Journal of Speech, 1933.

Although Negro speech is strikingly different from cultivated English, many of the differences are not easily reducible to phonetic terms. Wise summarizes the differences in vocabulary, conjugation, intonation, and placement, and lists the characteristics of the dialect that apply to the South at large.

Characteristics of Negro Speech

To a large degree, the Negro dialect, as it is spoken over practically the entire United States, is similar to the Southern dialect spoken by the uneducated whites. J. L. Dillard says that approximately eighty per cent of the Black population speak Black English. In addition, many members of the Puerto Rican community in New York City have learned Black English in addition to Puerto Rican Spanish. Dillard also says that Black English is the most homogeneous dialect of American English. [83] William A. Stewart suggests that there are structural differences in Negro and white dialects. [84] Stewart mentions several phonological and paralinguistic features that seem to be markers of Negro social dialect as well as a number of syntactic constructions which seem to have an ethnic distribution. Of these he includes the zero copula, possession indicated without a possessive morpheme, and the use of the verb be as a time extension auxiliary.

In another connection, Stewart points out that such "Negro" patterns as the "zero copula," the "zero possessive," of "undifferentiated pronouns" should not be attributed to carelessness, laziness, or stupidity, but should be treated as "language patterns which have been in existence for generations and which their present users have acquired, from parent and peer, through a perfectly normal kind of language-learning process."[85] Stewart also suggests that word-form similarities between non-standard Negro dialects and non-standard white dialects may be the result of a merging process in which creole-speaking Negroes tried to make their English become more like that of the whites by means of minor pronunciation changes and vocabulary substitutions, but that the grammatical patterns remained more resistant to this process. He thinks that further grammatical study

of non-standard Negro dialect may show many more differences between Negro and white speech patterns, differences
that may turn out to be traceable to a creole English, pidgin English, or even an African language source. [86]

Raven I. McDavid, Jr. , and Virginia Glenn McDavid
conclude that the overwhelming bulk of American Negro
speech, in vocabulary as well as in grammar and phonology,
is borrowed from the speech of the whites with whom Negroes have come in contact, but that the borrowing has also
gone in the other direction. They point out evidence of this
in vocabulary and mention that many whites along the South
Carolina coast have taken for as the particle for the infinitive of purpose. They also mention phonological elements
adopted by the whites, especially the tendency in Southern
speech to simplify final consonant clusters. [87]

Lee Pederson, Grace S. Reuter, and Joan H. Hall
observe in their study of the speech of North Georgia that
although black speech differed from white speech in all of
the twenty-five communities studied, on the basis of statistical incidence and "comprehensive patterning of recessive
forms, " no variety of black speech can be characterized
here as uniform or exclusive in terms of its segmental units.
Its uniqueness seems to rest in the position it occupies in
the rural community since it shares phonological features
with cultured blacks and whites, grammatical features with
white folk speakers, and lexical forms with all members of
both groups. [88]

Negro Dialect in Literature

Negro dialect appeared in American literature almost
at the same time as the Negro character. The first use of
Negro dialect in American literature is thought to be in The
Fall of British Tyranny by John Leacock, published in 1776.
According to Richard Walser, there are ten plays written before 1800 that have some relevance to the character of the
American Negro and to his dialect. [89] None of the playwrights,
he says, with the exception of John Murdock, exhibits any
great consistency in presenting the dialect. He concludes:
"However, whatever the origin, or whatever the influence
shaping the dialect, there are in these early dramatic ef-
forts the first consistent, though fumbling, attempts to trans-
late the spoken sounds and sentences into written words. The
plays provide us with definite proof that Negro dialect in

eighteenth-century America possessed a distinctiveness that
has never been lost.   They mark the beginnings of a literature of Negro dialect which eventually was to become a characteristic of much of the indigenous American writing. "90

The early writing about the Negro by white writers
stereotyped him as a contented slave or as a comic character seen at this best in minstrel shows.   These interpretations were followed by writers such as Irwin Russell and
Joel Chandler Harris who were interested in presenting the
folkways of the Negro.   In the twentieth century, the Negro
has been both romanticized and over-dramatized by white
writers, but, in the main, literature about the Negro reflects
the general social attitude towards him.   Lorraine Hansberry
says that the Negro as primarily presented in the past has
never existed on land or sea.   "It has seldom been a portrait of men, only a portrait of a concept, and that concept
has been a romance and no other thing.... It is a matter
of a partially innocent cultural heritage that, out of its own
needs, was eager to believe in the colossal charm, among
other things of 'childlike' peoples.   From that notation, pre-
sumably, came the tendency to find non-Negro dramatic and
musical materials rendered 'quaint' when performed by 'all-
colored casts. ' ... It is also interesting to note, in view of
the hoped-for transition, that these translations 'to the Negro' have generally meant ... haphazardly assaulting the English language beyond recognition, as if the Negro people had
not produced an idiom that has a real and specific character,
which is not merely the random exclusion of verb endings. "91

The Negro writer has been present since colonial days.
His early writing follows the patterns of his white contemporaries, for the fictional image had to be acceptable to his
readers.   Gradually such writers as Charles W. Chesnutt and
Paul Laurence Dunbar found acceptance and paved the way for
writers who have increased in number and in importance until at the present time a creditable amount of good literature
in various forms has been produced.   Thirty-odd novels were
written by Negroes before 1920, 92 and since that time have
appeared many excellent volumes by Negro writers.   Some
of the best of dialect writing is included in their productions.

Negro Dialect Used in Literature by White Writers

Edgar Allan POE (1809-1849), short story writer, poet,
and critic, was associate editor of the Southern Literary Mes-

senger, 1835-1837, and editor, associate editor, and contributor to such periodicals as Graham's and Burton's Gentleman's
Magazine, 1838-1843.   Erick Stockton says that despite his
other traits, Jupiter in "The Gold Bug" must "stand or fall
because of his dialect. "   His linguistic inconsistencies are
minor and even add to its truthfulness. 93   But Killis Campbell says that Jupiter's speech is badly managed. 94   "The
Gold Bug" appeared originally in The Philadelphia Dollar
Newspaper, June 21-28, 1843.

Sidney LANIER and Clifford LANIER (1844-1908).
For a short biographical account of Sidney Lanier, see
page 72.

Works:

"Uncle Jim's Baptist Revival Hymn, " in Poems of
Sidney Lanier.   Edited by His Wife.   New York: Charles
Scribner's Sons, 1906, pp. 175-176.   Originally published
in Scribner's Monthly, 1876.

"The Power of Prayer; Or, the First Steamboat up
the Alabama, " Scribner's Monthly, X (June, 1875), 239-240.
In Poems of Sidney Lanier, pp. 185-188.

Irwin RUSSELL (1853-1879), a native of Port Gibson,
Mississippi, is generally conceded to be the first Southern
writer to use all Negro characters in a literary production,
but in his use of Negro dialect in verse he is superseded in
time by Thomas Dunn English and by Sidney Lanier and his
brother Clifford. 95   In his introduction to the first edition
of Russell's collected poems (1888), Joel Chandler Harris
says: "Irwin Russell was among the first--if not the very
first--of Southern writers to appreciate the literary possi-
bilities of the Negro Character, and of the unique relations
existing between the two races before the war, and was a-
mong the first to develop them.... But the most wonderful
thing about the dialect poetry of Irwin Russell is his accurate conception of the Negro character.   The dialect is not
always the best, --it is often carelessly written, --but the
Negro is there, the old-fashioned, unadulterated Negro, who
is dear to the Southern heart. "

Works:

Christmas Night in the Quarters. New York: The
Century Company, 1888. First published in Scribner's
Monthly, 1878.

Joel Chandler HARRIS. For a brief account of the
life of Harris, see pages 57-8. For a discussion of the dialect
used by Harris, see Sumner Ives, "Dialect Differentiation in
the Stories of Joel Chandler Harris," page 23. Harris's chief
contribution to literature is his stories of Uncle Remus, told
in the language of the Negro. William Stanley Braithwaite
says: "Of all the American writers of this period, Joel
Chandler Harris has made the most permanent contribution
in dealing with the Negro. There is in his work both a
deepening of interest and technique. Here at least we have
something approaching true portraiture. "96

Works:

Uncle Remus: His Songs and His Sayings, The Folk-
lore of the Old Plantation (1880). New and revised edition.
With one hundred and twelve illustrations by A. B. Frost.
New York and London: D. Appleton and Company, 1930.

Nights with Uncle Remus: Myths and Legends of the
Old Plantation (1883). Boston: Houghton Mifflin Company, 1911.

Ruth McEnery STUART (1852-1917) was born in Louisiana but moved to Arkansas in 1879 after her marriage to a
planter. She wrote numerous volumes of short stories,
mainly of the post-Civil War South.

Works:

A Golden Wedding and Other Tales, 1893. Reprinted
by Books for Libraries Press, 1972. 366 pp.

"Aunt Delphi's Dilemma," 1891, in American Local-
Color Stories. Edited with an Introduction by Harry R. War-
fel and G. Harrison Orions. New York: Cooper Square
Publishers, Inc., 1970, pp. 735-743.

Thomas Nelson PAGE (1853-1922) was born at "Oakland," Hanover County, Virginia. He attended Washington

and Lee University, studied law, and settled in Richmond.
He reproduced the speech of the Negroes of Eastern Virginia. Page says in an introductory note to In Ole Virginia
that the dialect of the Negroes of Eastern Virginia is different from that of the Southern Negroes. He mentions particularly constant elision; the loss of final consonant in pronunciation; the slighting of adjectives, prepositions, and the possessive; and the pronunciation of r as ah.

Works:

In Ole Virginia, Marse Chan, and Other Stories. New
York: Charles Scribner's Sons, 1887. Six stories, five told
in dialect.

Elsket, and Other Stories, 1891. Reprinted by Books
for Libraries Press, 1969. 208 pp.

Pastime Stories. Illustrated by A. B. Frost, 1894.
Reprinted by Books for Libraries Press, 1969. 220 pp.
Twenty-three stories.

Samuel Minturn PECK (1854-1938) was born in Tus-
caloosa, Alabama. His parents moved to Illinois in 1865
but returned to Alabama in 1867. He attended the University
of Alabama and received an M. A. degree in 1876. He studied medicine at Bellevue College, New York.

Works:

Alabama Sketches. Chicago: A. C. McClurg and
Company, 1902. Reprinted by Books for Libraries Press,
1972. Includes eleven stories, two of which are in Negro
dialect; "The Trouble at St. James's, " and "The Old Piano. "

John Trotwood MOORE (1858-1929) was a native of
Alabama but lived most of his life in Tennessee. He was
associated with Robert Love Taylor in the Taylor-Trotwood
Magazine and served for many years as the state historian
of Tennessee. For a time he lived in Maury County, Tennessee, where he raised fine-blooded race horses.

Works:

Old Mistis and Other Songs and Stories from Tennessee

(1897). Nashville: The Cokesbury Press, 1925. 358 pp.

Songs and Stories from Tennessee (1902). Illustrated
by Howard Weeden and Robert Dickey. Reprinted by Books
for Libraries Press, 1969. 358 pp.

Uncle Wash, His Stories. Philadelphia: John C. Winston Company, 1910. 329 pp. Thirty-two stories.

Thomas DIXON, Jr. (1864-1946) was a native of
Shelby, North Carolina. He received his college training at
Wake Forest College, Greensboro Law School, and Johns
Hopkins University. He served in the North Carolina Legis-
lature for one year but resigned to enter the ministry. He
wrote novels and plays.

Works:

The Leopard's Spots. Doubleday, Page and Company,
1902. Reprinted by the Gregg Press, Inc., 1967. 469 pp.

The Clansman. Doubleday, Page and Company, 1905.
Republished by The Gregg Press, Inc., 1967. 374 pp.

Ridgely TORRENCE (1875-1950) was born in Xenia,
Ohio, and educated at Miami University and at Princeton U-
niversity. He served for a time as librarian of the Astor
Library in New York City. He is best known for his poetry
but he also wrote several plays.

Works:

"The Rider of Dreams," 1917; "Granny Maumee,"
1914; "Simon the Cyrenian," 1917. These plays were published as Three Plays of the Negro Theatre. New York:
Macmillan Company, 1917. "The Rider of Dreams" and
"Granny Maumee" are included in Plays of Negro Life.
Edited by Alain Locke and Montgomery Gregory. Illustrated by Aaron Douglas. New York: Harper and Brothers, 1927.

R. Emmet KENNEDY wrote stories of Negro life in
East Green, a Negro settlement in Gretna, a small town
across the Mississippi River from New Orleans.

Works:

Black Cameos.   New York: Albert and Charles Boni,
1924.   Short stories.

Gritney People, 1927.   Short stories.

Red Bean Row, 1929.   A novel.

Roark BRADFORD (1896-1948), a descendant of Gov-
ernor Bradford of Massachusetts, was born in Lauderdale
County, Tennessee.   He attended the University of California,
served as a lieutenant in the coast artillery during World
War I, and worked as a newspaper reporter in Atlanta and
New Orleans before he decided to devote his entire time to
writing.
    Bradford was the owner of Little Bee Bend Plantation
in northern Louisiana and knew well the speech of the Negroes he portrays in his writings.   In writing about Bradford after his death, David L. Cohn, a native of Greenville,
Mississippi, and his close friend, tells of his contact with
the people he wrote about: "They [the Negroes] looked upon
Brad, adjudged him good, and told him to set down, suh,
and scuse me whilst I gits another chunk of wood to th'ow
on this fire.   And sitting there, by many a cabin hearth, on
steamboats that plied the Mississippi, the Ouachita, the Red,
in prison camps, stores, schools, and churches, he found
the material for a shelf of books about the people with whom
he sat and (in collaboration with Marc Connelly) one of the
most distinguished plays that has graced the American stage--
"The Green Pastures. "97

Works:

Ol' Man Adam an' His Chillun.   New York and London: Harper and Brothers, Publishers, 1928.

This Side of Jordan.   Negro Life in Lower Mississippi,
1929.

Ol' King David an' the Philistine Boys, 1930.

John Henry, 1931.

    Marc CONNELLY (1890-   ) is a native of McKees-
port, Pennsylvania.   He collaborated with George S. Kaufman

on several plays before he took some of the stories of Roark
Bradford's Ol' Man Adam an' His Chillun, 1928, and turned
them into The Green Pastures, 1930, a mixture of story,
drama, and Negro spirituals, designed to show, in Connelly's
words, "the search of God for man, and man's search for
God." An account of his writing The Green Pastures, its
production, and reception in both the United States and Europe is given in Voices Offstage, A Book of Memoirs, by
Marc Connelly, 1968, pp. 144-198. See also John L. Phil-
lips. "Before the Colors Fade: Green Pastures Recalled,"
American Heritage, XXI (February, 1970), 28-29, 74-76.

Works:

The Green Pastures, in Sixteen Famous American
Plays. Edited by Bennett A. Cerf and Van H. Cartmell.
Random House, Inc., 1941. Modern Library Edition, pp.
147-159.

Eugene O'NEILL (1888-1953) was born in New York
City, the son of James O'Neill, an actor who became famous
for his acting in The Count of Monte Cristo. After touring
with his father's acting company and attending various board-
ing schools, O'Neill entered Princeton but did not complete
the freshman year. He worked at various jobs, went to
Honduras in search of gold, and in 1910 shipped in a freight-
er bound for Buenos Aires. He returned to New York and
lived for a time in a waterfront dive. In 1912 he was sent
to a tuberculosis sanitarium. During the six months that he
was confined in the sanitarium, O'Neill began to write plays.
Feeling the need of technical help, he attended George Pierce
Baker's 47 Workshop during the 1914-1915 term.
After spending the winter of 1915-1916 in Greenwich
Village, O'Neill became associated with the Provincetown
Players. This group produced many of his early plays. By
1920 he had produced Beyond the Horizon, his first full-length
play, which won him the Pulitzer Prize, and had thus estab-
lished himself as a dramatist. Anna Christie, 1921, and
Strange Interlude, 1928, were also awarded the Pulitzer Prize.
In 1936, O'Neill received the Nobel Prize for Literature. Before his death, he had published some two dozen plays. Long
Day's Journey into Night was produced posthumously in 1956.
Eleanor Flexner says of O'Neill's language: "His feeling for the language of our times in its crudest forms, for
the argot of poverty and ignorance and brutality that boils out
of the slums, out of the heart of living and action, is nothing

short of magnificent; here his writing attains the level of the first rate and comes the nearest he ever achieves to poetry. "[98] Ruby Cohn comments on the devices used by O'Neill to create tension in Emperor Jones and concludes with a statement about his dialogue in this play. "But dialogue remains O'Neill's major theatrical instrument. During the six Expressionist scenes Jones delivers a monologue that grows more feverish as time passes. Jones has all the language on stage as opposed to the 'h'ants'--mechanical Jeff, the automation chain gang, the 'marionettish' 1850 planters. As Jones retreats further into his past, his bursts of speech grow shorter; by Scene 7 he echoes the chant of the Witch Doctor 'without articulate word division. ' The American Negro is finally absorbed by a preverbal magic of his racial inheritance; nothing remains of the rational robber-emperor. In the final scene West Indian Lem tolls a verbal knell for Jones with four repetitions of 'We cotch him. '"[99]

Works:

The Emperor Jones, produced November 1, 1920. Copyright, 1921. In Three Plays by Eugene O'Neill. Introduction by Lionel Trilling. New York: Random House. Modern Library Edition.

The Dreamy Kid, produced October 31, 1919. Copyright, 1920, by Eugene O'Neill and Theatre Arts Monthly; 1924, by Boni and Liveright. In Plays of Negro Life. Selected and edited by Alain Locke and Montgomery Gregory. New York: Harper and Brothers, 1927, pp. 1-24.

Paul GREEN. For a short biographical account of Paul Green, see page 75.

Works:

"The No 'Count Boy, " A Folk Comedy in One Act (1925), and "White Dresses" (1920), in Plays of Negro Life. Edited by Alain Locke and Montgomery Gregory. New York: Harper and Brothers, 1927, pp. 69-96, 117-138.

Negro Dialect Used in Literature by Negro Writers

Charles W. CHESNUTT (1858-1932) was born in Cleveland, Ohio, the son of a prosperous farmer. When he was eight, the family moved to Fayetteville, North Carolina, where Chesnutt grew up. He began his writing career with the publication of "The Goophered Grapevine" in the Atlantic Monthly, 1887. This story was later used as the first story of The Conjure Woman, seven stories told in dialect by Uncle Julian, a former slave who uses his stories of conjuring among the Negroes to help achieve his own desires.

Works:

The Conjure Woman. Boston: Houghton, Mifflin and Company, 1899. Republished by The Gregg Press, Inc., 1968. 229 pp.

The Wife of His Youth, and Other Stories of the Color Line. Boston: Houghton, Mifflin and Company, 1899. Reprinted by University of Michigan Press, 1968.

The House Behind the Cedars, novel. Boston: Houghton, Mifflin and Company, 1900.

The Marrow of Tradition, novel. Boston: Houghton, Mifflin and Company, 1901.

The Colonel's Dream, novel. New York: Doubleday, Page and Company, 1905. Republished by The Gregg Press, 1968. 294 pp.

James Edwin CAMPBELL (1867-1895) is considered to be the first Black poet to write in Black plantation dialect. He was born in Pomeroy, Ohio. After graduating from Pomeroy Academy in 1884, he taught for two years at Buck Ridge, Ohio. He became head of the Langston School in Point Pleasant, West Virginia, and in 1892, of the West Virginia Colored Institute. He became a journalist in Chicago and probably wrote his dialect poetry while working in Chicago. J. Saunders Redding says: "Campbell's dialect is more nearly a reproduction of plantation Negro speech sounds than that of any other writer in American literature.... Campbell's ear alone dictated his language."[100] James Weldon Johnson says that Campbell's "dialect, idiomatically and phonetically, is nearer to the Gullah or to the West Indian dialect. His use of the broad 'a' and of the objective form of the personal pronouns for the nominative is not in accord with the pronunciation and mode of speech used generally by the Negro in the United States for, at least, the past half century.   There is more than a slight similarity between his earlier poems and the poems of Claude McKay in the West Indian dialect. "101

Works:

Echoes from the Cabin and Elsewhere, his second volume of poems.   1895.   86 pp.

Paul Laurence DUNBAR (1872-1906) was born in Dayton, Ohio, the son of former slaves.   After graduating from high school, he took a job as an elevator boy in a Dayton hotel.   His first book was privately printed and the publishing costs paid for by Dunbar through the sale of copies while he worked as an elevator operator.   In 1897 he went to England and upon his return was given a position in the Library of Congress, Washington, D. C.

Dunbar wrote four volumes of short stories and four novels, but he is best known for his poetry.   Lyrics of Lowly Life, 1896, with an introduction by William Dean Howells, became his best-known book.   James Weldon Johnson says of Dunbar: "There have been many changes in the estimates of Negro poetry since Dunbar died, but he still holds his place as the first American Negro poet of real literary distinction. ...   In the field in which he became best known, Negro dialect poetry, his work has not been excelled. "

Works:

Lyrics of Lowly Life.   Introduction by William Dean Howells.   New York: Dodd, Mead and Company, 1896.

Lyrics of the Hearthside, 1899.

Lyrics of Love and Laughter, 1903.

Lyrics of Sunshine and Shadow, 1905.

James Weldon JOHNSON (1871-1936) was born in Jacksonville, Florida.   He graduated from Atlanta University and received an M. A. degree from Columbia University.   He began teaching at the Stanton School in Jacksonville, where he later became the principal.   After a short time, he studied law and became the first Negro since Reconstruction to be admitted to the bar in Florida through open examination.

He soon lost interest in law and turned to music. With his brother, John Rosamond, he began to write songs for Tin Pan Alley. Later he turned to politics and served seven years as United States counsul in Venezuela and Nicaragua. He was secretary for the National Association for the Advancement of Colored People for fourteen years. In 1930 he became Professor of Creative Literature at Fisk University. In 1938, he was killed in an automobile accident while vacationing in Maine.

Works:

Fifty Years and Other Poems. Introduction by Brander Matthews. Boston: The Cornhill Company, 1917. 93 pp. Contains a section of dialect poems under the title of "Jingles and Croons," about one-third of the collection.

Jean TOOMER (1894-1967) was born in Washington, D. C., of New Orleans Creole ancestry. He studied at the University of Wisconsin and at the City College of New York. He lived for a short time with artists and writers of Carmel, California, and at Taos, New Mexico, but finally became a Quaker in Bucks County, Pennsylvania. He taught in the schools of Sparta, Georgia, for a time, an experience that gave him the background for his novel.

Works:

Cane. New York: Boni and Liveright, 1923. Perennial Classics Edition. Introduction by Arna Bontemps, 1969. 239 pp. Cane is a collection of prose pieces interspersed with poems and concluding with a closet drama. Some dialect is used.

Balo. A One-Act Sketch of Negro Life. New York: Boni and Liveright, 1924. Reprinted in Plays of Negro Life. Edited by Alain Locke and Montgomery Gregory. New York: Harper and Brothers, 1927, pp. 269-286.

Rudolph FISHER (1897-1934) was born in Washington, D. C., but was brought up in Providence, Rhode Island. He received two degrees from Brown University and then entered Howard University Medical School, graduating in 1924 with the highest honors. While in medical school, Fisher began to write short stories that appeared in such journals as the

Atlantic Monthly, McClure's, Opportunity, and Story. He later wrote two novels.

Works:

Stories: "High Yeller," Crisis, 1925; "City of Refuge" and "Ring Tail," Atlantic Monthly, 1925; "The Promised Land" and "Blades of Steel," Atlantic Monthly, 1927; "Guardian of the Law," Opportunity, 1933; "Miss Cynthie," Story, 1933.

The Walls of Jericho, novel. New York: Knopf, 1928; Arno Press, 1969. 293 pp. 12 pages of "Introduction to Contemporary Harlemese."

The Conjure Man Dies, novel. New York: Covici, Friede, 1932.

Langston HUGHES (1902-1967) was born in Joplin, Missouri, graduated from high school in Cleveland, Ohio, and enrolled at Columbia University. He left Columbia to go to sea as a messboy. After leaving the sea, he entered Lincoln University, graduating in 1929. He became a leader in the Harlem Renaissance and earned for himself the unofficial title as "the Poet Laureate of the Negro People." Hughes is one of the most prolific of Negro writers. His publications include thirty-nine volumes of his own, five adult books in collaboration, four full-length translated works, hundreds of uncollected pieces, and several edited collections of Negro literature. His list includes sixty-six published short stories, more than twenty dramas, operas, musical, and gospel song-plays, his autobiography in two parts, thirteen volumes of verse, and several novels.

"The astonishing feature of Langston Hughes' art is his unerring re-creation of the imagery, idiom, and syntax of black speech. This was not the result of chance, for Hughes' own spontaneous speech was quite different from that of the folk. His achievement was that of a connoisseur in love with the speech of black folk and with the folk themselves."102

Works:

Short stories: The Ways of White Folks, 1934; Laughing to Keep from Crying, 1952; Something in Common, 1963.

Poetry: The Dream Keeper, with Illustrations by Helen Sewell. New York: Alfred A. Knopf, 1932. 77 pp. Includes a few dialect poems.

The Weary Blues. Introduction by Carl Van Vechten. New York: Alfred A. Knopf, 1926. 109 pp. Includes several dialect poems.

Fine Clothes to the Jew. New York: Alfred A. Knopf, 1927.

Shakespeare in Harlem. New York: Alfred A. Knopf, 1947. Includes several dialect poems.

Novels: Not Without Laughter. New York: Alfred A. Knopf, 1930. 324 pp.

Tambourines to Glory. New York: Hill and Wang, 1958.

Play: Mulatto, 1935.

Arna BONTEMPS (1902-1973) was born in Alexandria, Louisiana, but grew up in California. He graduated from Pacific Union College in 1923 and the next year went to Harlem. In the 1920's he won several prizes for poetry. In the next decade he wrote short stories, three novels, and two books for children. He also taught school in Alabama and in Chicago. He studied at Columbia University and at the University of Chicago and then became head librarian at Fisk University in 1944. He became writer in residence at Fisk in 1970. Bontemps wrote more than twenty-five books, many of them children's books and black historical fiction. With Countee Cullen, he wrote the book for the Mercer-Arlen Broadway musical, St. Louis Woman, 1946, based on his novel God Sends Sunday, 1931.

Works:

God Sends Sunday, novel. New York: Harcourt, Brace and Company, 1931.

Black Thunder, novel. New York: Macmillan Company, 1936; Berlin: Seven Seas Paperback, 1964. 224 pp.

Zora Neale HURSTON (1903-1960) was born in Eaton-
ville, Florida, the first all-Negro town to be incorporated in
the United States. She attended high school at Morgan Academy of Morgan College, Baltimore. After one year at Howard University, she transferred to Barnard College, where
she majored in anthropology with Franz Boas. She received
a B.A. degree in 1928 and was awarded a fellowship at Columbia University to work toward a Ph.D. degree in anthropology. She did not complete the degree but decided to write
realistically about her own people. She received a fellowship
from the Rosenwald Foundation in 1915 and Guggenheim fel-
lowships in 1936 and 1937 to study native customs in Haiti.
She taught drama for a time at North Carolina College in
Durham. Several of her stories were published in periodicals.

Works:

Stories: "Spunk," Opportunity, August, 1926, prize-
winning story; "Muttsy," Opportunity, August, 1926; "Sweat,"
Fire, I, November, 1926; "The Gilded Six-Bits," published
in Story, August, 1933.

Jonah's Gourd Vine. Philadelphia: J. B. Lippincott,
1934.

Mules and Men. Introduction by Darwin T. Turner.
Philadelphia: J. B. Lippincott, 1935. Reprinted in Perennial Library Edition, 1970. 343 pp.

Their Eyes Were Watching God. Philadelphia: J. B.
Lippincott, 1937. Fawcett Premier Book Edition, 1965.
159 pp.

Richard WRIGHT (1908-1960) was born on a farm
near Natchez, Mississippi. He grew up in Memphis, Tennessee, but went to live in Chicago at an early age. His
first collection of stories was published in 1938, but it was
Native Son, a novel, that brought him to national attention.
After World War II, he went to Paris, where he lived until
his death.

Works:

Uncle Tom's Children, four novellas. New York and
London: Harper and Brothers, 1938. 317 pp. Second edition in 1940 includes five stories.

Eight Men, short stories, 1940. New York: Pyramid Books, 1961.

Native Son. New York: Harper and Brothers, 1940. 359 pp. Reprinted, 1966. Made into a play in ten scenes by Paul Green and Richard Wright, 1941.

James W. BUTCHER, Jr. (1909-   ) was born in Washington, D. C. He attended Howard University for three years but received the B. A. degree from the University of Illinois and an M. A. degree from the University of Iowa.

Works:

"The Seer, " in The Negro Caravan. Selected and Edited by Sterling A. Brown, Arthur P. Davis, and Ulysses Lee. New York: The Dryden Press, 1941, pp. 520-534.

Margaret WALKER (Mrs. F. J. Alexander) (1915-   ) was born in Birmingham, Alabama. She graduated with a B. A. degree from Northwestern University and received both M. A. and Ph. D. degrees from the University of Iowa. She has won numerous prizes and awards.

Works:

For My People. New Haven: Yale University Press, 1942. Includes some poems in dialect.

Jubilee. Boston: Houghton Mifflin Company, 1966. 497 pp.

Thomas D. PAWLEY, Jr. (1917-   ) was born in Jackson, Mississippi. He was educated at Virginia State College and at the University of Iowa.

Works:

Jedgment Day, 1938, included in The Negro Caravan. Selected and edited by Sterling A. Brown, Arthur P. Davis, and Ulysses Lee. New York: Dryden Press, 1941, pp. 534-543.

Ernest J. GAINES (1933-   ) was born on a plantation near Oscar, Louisiana. When he was fifteen, his family moved to Vallejo, California. After two years in the
Army, he enrolled in San Francisco State College, graduating in 1957. He won a fellowship to Stanford University in
1958 to study creative writing. The following year he received the Joseph Henry Jackson Literary Award for a draft
of his first novel, Barren Summer, which he completed in
1963. He has been given numerous awards and grants for
his writing.

Works:

Barren Summer, 1963.

Catherine Carmier, 1964. New York: Atheneum,
1967.

Of Love and Lust, 1967. Bantam, 1969.

Bloodline, a collection of stories, 1968. Includes
"The Sky Is Gray," which first appeared in Negro Digest,
August, 1963.

The Autobiography of Miss Jane Pittman, a novel.
New York: The Dial Press, 1971.

Records in the Negro Dialect

In Abraham's Bosom and Roll Sweet Chariot. Read
by Paul Green. After a discussion of folk and symphonic
drama, Green reads from these works. Spoken Arts, No.
719. Spoken Arts, Inc., Box 542, New Rochelle, N.Y.

Anthology of Negro Poets. Edited by Arna Bontemps.
(Poems read by Langston Hughes, Sterling Brown, Claude
McKay, Countee Cullen, etc.) Folkways Records, FP91.

Anthology of Negro Poets in the U.S.A. for 200 Years.
Read by Arna Bontemps. Folkways Records, FP 91-92.

The Dream Keeper and Other Poems of Langston
Hughes. Read by the Author. Folkways Records, FP 104.

Four Readings from "God's Trombones." Read by
James Weldon Johnson. Musicraft Album, No. 21. ("List-

en, Lord, " "The Creation, " "Go Down, Death, " "The Prod-
igal. ")

"... And this language [Gullah] which is not easily understood by a trained ear, is not only beautiful, but its whimsical words and phrases, its quaint similes and shrewd sayings are undoubtedly a permanent enrichment of American language and literature. "

--Julia Peterkin, "Gullah, " in Ebony and Topaz, a Collectanea. Edited by Charles S. Johnson. Freeport, N. Y. : Books for Libraries Press, 1971, p. 35. First published, 1927.

THE GULLAH DIALECT

Historical Background

Gullah, also called Geechee (from the Ogeechee River near Savannah), is the language spoken by the descendants of slaves and by some whites in a modified form[103] in the region extending along the Atlantic coast approximately from Georgetown, South Carolina to the northern boundary of Florida.[104] The language is a creolized form of the English spoken by the slaves who were brought to this region during the eighteenth and the first half of the nineteenth century, mixed with survivals of their native African languages. The slaves were brought in large numbers directly from Africa to work on the rice and indigo plantations on the so-called Sea Islands, for it was commonly thought that the climate in these regions was certain death for white people. The slaves lived in almost complete isolation with little contact with white men until after the Civil War.[105]

John Bennett, a native of Ohio who made his home in Charlestown, South Carolina, is one of the first students of Gullah. He says that the vocabulary of Gullah is English but that the intonation may be African, and although the number of African words, phrases, and idioms is comparatively small, these joined with the intonation and the amount of folklore involved cause the Gullah to be more African than other Negro dialects.[106] He also says that "its strange words, singular pronunciations, peculiar corruptions, and frequent abbreviations so disguise the familiar features of one's native tongue, while rhythmical modulations and unfamiliar accents, characteristics of some European languages, give it so un-English a sound that a stranger, upon first hearing, might, indeed frequently does, mistake it for some foreign tongue." Bennett also says that some of the plantations were so remote that dialects developed within the dialect. It was possible to determine by his peculiarity of speech, the plantation to which a Negro belonged.

Guy S. Johnson says that Gullah can be traced in practically every detail to English dialect sources. [107] He maintains that both the Negro and the Southern White spoke the language they learned from the white settlers. The early seventeenth-century settlers spoke dialect English rather than Standard English. Many of these settlers were laborers and artisans who worked side by side with Negro slaves, and it was from these settlers that the slaves learned most of their English. This was particularly true in the period before large plantations were developed. Johnson thinks that the second source of the peculiarities of Gullah is the "baby talk" the overseers used with the slaves--a simplification of tense, inflections, gender, number, etc.--to make communication easier. He thinks that Gullah was probably fairly well established before the large plantation system came into existence. The new slaves acquired their language from the older Negroes. After the Civil War, many of the Negroes remained where they were and their isolation kept their language more or less unchanged. Johnson concludes that Gullah "is as different from what is generally thought of as Negro dialect as the speech of the white Georgian is from that of the Chicagoan. With its rapidly spoken phrases, its staccato accents, and its rising and falling intonations, it sounds to the average American more like French or Spanish than any English he has ever heard. "[108]

Bennett points out that students of Gullah have noticed certain minor variations in phonology and vocabulary in the language used on different islands. "Phrases heard on the Altamaha are unknown upon the Santee; words in use in the Georgetown District vanish at Edisto; John's Island is not St. Helena's; Silk Hope was not Toogoodoo. Yet all the remote varieties blend into one generic tongue under the common name of Gullah. "[109] These differences he attributes to the variety of backgrounds represented by the colonial families and to the assimilation of these varieties by the slaves. Johnson says that there is considerable variation in the printed records of Gullah dialects. [110] These variations are due in part to the local and individual variations in phonology and in part to the recorders who found it difficult to record accurately what Johnson calls "a mouth-full-of-mush effect, rolling out ... short-clipped words with a rapidity which is amazing to those who think that all Negroes drawl. " Johnson commends the recordings of Charles Colcomb Jones, Jr., Ambrose E. Gonzales, and Marcellus S. Whaley, but he says that Mrs. A. M. H. Christensen and Mrs. Elsie Clews Parsons collected their stories from people who spoke a modified Gullah.

Ambrose E. Gonzales calls the territory about a hundred miles wide along the seacoast from Georgetown, South Carolina into Georgia, known locally as the "Low Country," the "Black Border." He says of the Gullahs:

> Slovenly and careless of speech, these Gullahs
> seized upon the peasant English used by some of
> the early settlers and by the white servants of the
> wealthier Colonists, wrapped their clumsy tongues
> about it as well as they could, and, enriched with
> certain expressive African words, it issued through
> their flat noses and thick lips as so workable a
> form of speech that it was gradually adopted by the
> other slaves and became in time the accepted Ne-
> gro speech of the lower districts of South Carolina
> and Georgia. [111]

Johnson points out that if the nearly two-thousand words Gonzales lists in The Black Border (Glossary, pp. 287-340) as words commonly used in the Gullah dialect in the Edisto Island region, are divided arbitrarily into appropriate classes, 92 per cent will be Standard English words pronounced in the standard way or as pronounced in the English dialect of the eighteenth century; six per cent will be corruptions and mutilations of Standard English words; two per cent will be archaic and obsolescent English words; and less than .5 per cent will be African words. Johnson says that this distribution also hold good for Whaley's glossary of 1,500 words.

According to Lorenzo D. Turner, who investigated several West African languages as a means of studying Gullah and is one of the most important scholars of the language, Gullah reveals survivals from many of the African languages spoken by slaves who were brought to South Carolina and Georgia during the first half of the nineteenth century. These survivals are most numerous in the vocabulary but can also be observed in the sounds, syntax, morphology, and intonation. He says that there are also many striking similarities between Gullah and the African languages in the methods used to form words. [112] Turner says that Gullah is probably a corruption of Angola, the name of the district from which many of the Carolina Negroes were brought in the days of the slave trader. [113] Johnson, Reed Smith, and Bennett suggest another possible origin of the name, the name of the Liberian group of tribes known as the Golas or Goras, living on the West Coast between Sierre Leone and the Ivory Coast.

Julia Peterkin thinks that the slaves may have been brought from Gallah on the African east coast along with cargoes of salt, which was so valuable that it was once used as money currency. 114

Turner says that the conclusion of Bennett, Gonzales, and others that the African languages had little effect upon Gullah shows that these writers were not acquainted with the African languages spoken by the Negroes who were brought to South Carolina and Georgia, and that they were also un-acquainted with the languages and cultures of the Negroes in the Caribbean, Brazil, and other parts of the New World, and were thus seriously handicapped in trying to record a dialect which was to them strange and new. He says that of the approximately seventeen hundred words which Gonzales includes in his glossary, fewer than a dozen are African, and these few Gonzales interprets as English, even misspell-ing them to indicate the Negro's inability to pronounce them. Turner also says that the statements of Smith, Stoney and Shelby, as well as those of Johnson and Crum, indicate their lack of acquaintance with the African languages that influenced Gullah. He also discredits the "baby-talk" theory of Johnson.

Raven I. McDavid, Jr., and Virginia Glenn McDavid say that Turner's statement that an investigation of Gullah speech discloses several thousand items previously derived from the language of the parts of Africa from which the slaves were taken is impressive, but more important are the implied conclusions: that many structural features of Gullah are also to be found in creolized languages of South America and the Caribbean, in the trade English of West Africa, and in many African languages. They continue:

> Perhaps most significant of all, though hardly hinted at by Turner, is the evidence from phono-logical structure: like the languages of West Af-rica described by Westermann and Ward, Gullah has a far less complex system of vowel phonemes than any known variety of English; furthermore, Gullah has a remarkable uniformity, not only in phonemic structure but in the phonetic shape of vowel allophones, along a stretch of nearly four hundred miles of the South Atlantic coast, in the very region where there is a greater variety a-mong the dialects of white speech than one can find elsewhere in the English-speaking North Amer-

ica--a uniformity difficult to explain by chance, or
by any of the older explanations of Negro speech.[115]

Studies of the Gullah Dialect

1.   Marcel [W. F. Allen].   "The Negro Dialect," in
The Negro and His Folklore in Nineteenth-Century Periodicals.   Edited and with an Introduction by Bruce Jacks.   Austin: University of Texas Press, American Folklore Society,
1967, pp. 74-81.   Reprinted from Nation, I (December 14,
1865), 744-745.
     An account of Allen's observations of Negro speech
during a residence of some months on one of the Sea Island
plantations of Port Royal at the northern end of St. Helena
Island.   Allen analyzes the language as he observed it and
illustrates his statements with selections from the songs,
both hymns and shouts, of the Sea Island Negroes.   A de-
tailed discussion of the dialect of the Sea Island Negroes by
W. F. Allen is also given in the Introduction of Slave Songs
of the United States, edited by W. F. Allen, Charles Pickard
Ware, and Lucy McKim Garrison, 1867; reprinted Peter
Smith, 1951, pp. xxiii-xxxvi.

2.   Bascom, William R.   "Acculturation Among the
Gullah Negroes," in Perspectives on Black English.   Edited
by J. L. Dillard.   The Hague; Mouton and Company, 1975,
pp. 280-287.
     A paper read before the Central Section, American
Anthropological Association and printed originally in the
American Anthropologist, XLIII, No. 1 (1941), 43-50.   Bascom says that the differences in the general patterns of the
cultures of Africa and Europe were not great.   He assesses
the African influences on the culture of the Gullahs, mention-
ing particularly the African influence on the institutions of
cooperative work among the Gullahs as well as on such institutions as the matriarchal family life.   He also points out
that Gullah speech has a number of African idioms and grammatical peculiarities.

3.   Bennett, John.   "Gullah: A Negro Patois," The
South Atlantic Quarterly, VII (1908), 332-347; VIII (1909),
39-52.
     One of the early studies of the history of Gullah with
numerous illustrations of its strange words, pronunciations,
peculiar corruptions, and abbreviations.

4. Crum, Mason. "The Gullah Dialect," in Gullah: Negro Life in the Carolina Sea Islands. Durham, N. C.: Duke University Press, 1940. Ann Arbor, Mich.: University Microfilms, 1968, pp. 101-131.

Crum says that the area in which the Gullah dialect is spoken is the islands and coast of South Carolina beginning at Georgetown and extending south through Charleston, Savannah, and the Georgia coast. The most extreme form of the dialect is found in the neighborhood of Edisto Island and Cumbahee section. On the islands near Charleston and around Port Royal and St. Helena Islands the dialect has been modified by contacts with the urban centers. Crum summarizes the opinions of Gullah as given by John Bennett, Marcellus S. Whaley, and Reed Smith, and refers to the contributions to the use of Gullah in literature by DuBose Heyward, Julia Peterkin, Stoney and Shelby, Poe, William Gilmore Simms, and Ambrose E. Gonzales. He also mentions the contributions of the Northerners who were in the South during and immediately after the Civil War and discusses the stories and the folklore collected by Charles Colcock Jones, Jr., and Mrs. A. M. H. Christensen. He gives a list of Gullah words from the glossaries of Gonzales and Whaley, gives a few specimens of the dialect, and concludes with a five-page bibliography of works on Gullah and the background and history of the area.

5. Gonzales, Ambrose E. The Black Border. Gullah Stories of the Carolina Coast. Columbia, S. C.: The State Company, 1922. "Foreword," pp. 7-18; "A Gullah Glossary," pp. 277-286.

In the "Foreword," Gonzales traces the history of the slave trade to the mainland colonies of North America, discusses the Gullah dialect, and explains the use of Negro dialect by several American writers. In "A Gullah Glossary," Gonzales discusses the pronunciation of Gullah and lists some seventeen hundred words with their English meanings.

6. Johnson, Guy B. Folk Culture on St. Helena Island, South Carolina. Foreword by Dan Yoder, 1930; reprinted Hatboro, Pa.: Folklore Associates, Inc., 1968. 183 pp.

Johnson says that Gullah is the most African of our Negro dialects; yet it can be traced in practically every detail to English speech. He analyzes the dialect from the standpoints of phonology, grammar, and vocabulary. He concludes that the Negro in the low-country responded to the speech patterns with which he was confronted--that of the

early settlers who spoke dialect English. Thus his speech
is in many ways a duplicate of the eighteenth-century English
dialect. Later, the overseers on the plantations used a sort
of "baby-talk" to their slaves to simplify the language. Johnson thinks that the frequent and extensive change of pitch in
Gullah may come from West Africa.

7. Kane, Elisha K. "The Negro Dialects Along the
Savannah River," Dialect Notes, V (1918-1927), 354-367.
Kane distinguishes three dialects on the Savannah
River: the Gullah, which extends along the South Carolina
seaboard and up the Savannah River for about thirty miles;
the Swamp Nigger, which begins where the Gullah leaves off
and reaches to within forty miles of Augusta, Georgia; and a
small area of dialect which has no name. The main part of
the article is a phonetic transcription of the author's experiences in every-day dialect with the conversations first given
in type in the conventional spelling which writers of Negro
dialect use.

8. Nixon, Nell Marie. Gullah and Backwoods Dialect in Selected Works of William Gilmore Simms. Ph. D.
Dissertation, University of South Carolina, 1971. Ann Arbor, Mich.: University Microfilms, 1973. 283 pp.
Chapter I (106 pages) of this study is concerned with
an analysis of Simms's use of Gullah dialect in eight novels
and three stories from the collection, The Wigwam and the
Cabin. Included is a discussion of the origin and background
of Gullah dialect by students of the dialect. Simms's Gullah
dialect is examined for accuracy in phonology, morphology,
syntax, and vocabulary and its use compared with statements
of the Gullah dialect made by such students as Reed Smith,
Mason Crum, Ambrose E. Gonzales, Harold Wentworth, and
Lorenzo Dow Turner. Nixon concludes that Simms's Gullah
dialect is sufficiently accurate to be used as a reliable basis
for study of the dialect and provides evidence that the Negro
speech is almost wholly derived from the speech of white
illiterates who taught English to the Gullahs.

9. Smith, Reed. Gullah. Columbia, S. C.: University of South Carolina, Bulletin, No. 190, 1926. 45 pp.
Dedicated to the memory of Ambrose E. Gonzales.
A survey of the studies of the Gullah dialect and of
the stories and sketches using this particular language.

10. Stoddard, Albert H. "Origin, Dialect, Beliefs,
and Characteristics of the Negroes of the South Carolina and

Georgia Coasts," Georgia Historical Review, X (1944), 186-195.

Stoddard says that the bulk of the original slaves that were brought to the coasts of South Carolina and Georgia came from the West Coast of Africa, but their numbers were augmented by members of tribes from the interior. Thus there was a mixture of peoples of different tribes with various tribal characteristics and dialects. Other slaves were brought from the West Indies where their forbears had been brought by the Spaniards from Portuguese Angola. In the new country they learned English from their overseers or slaves that had preceded them. Thus their language that became known as Gullah is an adaptation of their African languages to that of English.

11. Stoney, Samuel Gaillard, and Gertrude Mathews Shelby. "The Family Tree of Gullah Folk Speech and Folk Tales," in Black Genesis, a Chronicle. New York: Macmillan Company, 1930, pp. ix-xxv.

Stoney and Shelby say that the branches of the family tree of Gullah are American, that the trunk is West Indian, and that the roots are English and African. Because of the demand for labor in the Antilles, men came from Great Britain and Ireland, some of their own account, some under indenture, and many in virtual slavery as a result of the political conditions. The remainder of the population was Negro, who spoke some variants of the Bantu language of Africa, and who were taught English in limited form and with a limited vocabulary. African inheritance survives in a number of rhymes, games, and systems of counting; in tricks of the tongue; and in a few words in common use.

12. Turner, Lorenzo Dow. Africanisms in the Gullah Dialect. Chicago: University of Chicago Press, 1949. New York: Arno Press, 1969. 317 pp.

Turner bases his study on interviews with speakers of the Gullah dialect in communities in coastal South Carolina and Georgia, phonograph recordings of many varieties of material in the same areas, and interviews with twenty-seven natives of French West Africa to determine the indebtedness of Gullah to African sources. He shows the sections of West Africa from which the slaves were brought to South Carolina and Georgia (page 7), lists the West African words in Gullah (pages 43-208), and compares the syntactical features, the morphological features, word-formations, the sounds and intonation of Gullah with those of the West African languages. These are followed by Gullah texts given in both Gullah and in phonetic notation. A bibliography on African languages and the Gullah dialect is included in an appendix.

13. Van Sertima, Ivan. "My Gullah Brother and I: Exploration into a Community's Language and Myth through Its Oral Tradition," in Black English, A Seminar. Edited by Deborah Sears Harrison and Tom Trabasso. Hillsdale, N. J. : Laurence Erlbaum Associates, Publishers, 1976, pp. 123-146.

An account by a native of Guyana, now an Assistant Professor at Douglass College, Rutgers University, of his work on Johns Island and James Island, and in Charleston, South Carolina, in the fall of 1970 and 1971, in an attempt to go beyond the work of Lorenzo Turner in Gullah studies and to bring Turner's work up-to-date. Van Sertima sought to demonstrate the African presence in the Gullah language through using old men and women of the islands as informants and through analysis of the African folktales told by the informants. He concludes his presentation by listing sixteen distinctions that he finds between Gullah and Standard English, distinctions that may also be viewed as a tentative outline of a Black English grammar.

14. Wilkinson, Lupton A. "Gullah versus Grammar," North American Review, CCXXXVI, No. 6 (December, 1933), 539-542.

An argument for improving English grammar by adapting the Gullah dialect process of simplification. Wilkinson cites an example given by Reed Smith of the Gullah sentence, "Uh yeddy (heard) um but uh ent shum," which has sixty-four interpretations and if each of the uh's is changed to 'e the sixty-four can be multiplied by three and the total again tripled. He comments on the way the Gullah makes new words and how he changes English words through phonetic associations as well as on his ability to form proverbs and adages and to apply his poetic gift to language.

Characteristics of the Gullah Dialect

Bennett says that Gullah is difficult to speak, hard to understand, impossible to read to one's self or aloud with readiness. "The ordinary reader may not always catch the meaning; the shapes of the words are strange; they are often the residuum of language literally worn away by use; the phonology is archaic; the engaged grammar a mystery; to

the wit and to the acute phonetic sense of the reader much
must inevitably be left. "116 He points out some of the peculiarities of the vocabulary. One is used to mean only, or
alone. Soon is synonymous with early. A common unit of
measurement of area and distance is a tass, a task. A done-
tass niggah is a worn-out negro laborer or one that has fin-
ished his day's work. Stand means to be or to exist. Clean
means entirely, completely: clean gone.

Bennett also mentions the shortening of words, the
elision of syllables, and the modification of difficult enunciation. Enty is ain't he; shum de-day means see it, him, them.
The title for white man is buckra or buckerra. This may be
'sho nuff buckra or Po' buckra. There is no distinction of
pronouns with regard to sex. The feminine and the possessive forms are rarely used. Bennett lists numerous examples
of Gullah words and pronunciations and concludes that Gullah
is "the oddest negro patois in America; the most African; un-
altered it is one of the oldest; if not the oldest, certainly it
is the most archaic; and well worth the scientific and scholarly study which has been given the dialects of the Mississippi Delta, of Haiti, and of Martinique. "117

Johnson says that a careful study of Gullah reveals
law and order in the seeming chaos of the dialect. 118 He
says that he has yet to find an example of pronunciation, except in individual cases, not easily explicable on the basis
of Midland and Southern English dialects. He points out some
of the peculiarities of the pronunciation and in most cases is
able to show to his own satisfaction their origin in English
dialects. He says that the Gullah grammar is merely simplified English grammar. Singular forms of nouns are used
for the plural (exceptions are mens and crabbies [crabs]).
The sign of the genitive is nearly always omitted. The nominative and objective forms of the personal pronouns are often reversed. "Him sent dis to we. " Um serves for her,
it, him, them. You is nearly always onna, woona, or yoona.
Verb endings are cut to the minimum with adjectives and nouns
freely converted into verbs. "De young gal pledjub [pleasure]
heself. "

Gonzales says that it is doubtful that the vocabulary
of any single individual comprises more than half his list of
nearly two thousand words and that many of the words are
known only in special localities. Various names for the same
objects may be found in different areas. He suggests that
anyone trying to understand Gullah must reckon with the sounds

"uh," ("bubbuh," "farruh," "mastuh," "ribbuh"), "e" (a contraction of he, she, it, and them). There are many contra-
dictions and many short cuts as well as ramblings in the language. "Um shum" may mean I saw him, I see him, I saw
her, I saw it, I see it, I saw them, I see them.

   Turner divides his list of West African words that he
finds in Gullah into three groups: Personal names, other
words used in conversation, and words heard only in songs,
stories, and prayers. The most striking similarities between Gullah and West African languages, he finds, are revealed in the absence of any distinction in voice, in the em-
ployment of verb phrases, in the use of to be as a verb of
incomplete predication, in the comparison of adjectives, in
the use of verbal adjectives, in word order, and in frequent
repetition of words and phrases throughout the sentence.
Turner also notices many striking resemblances of Gullah to
several West African languages in the sounds as well as in
the intonation patterns. (See Turner, Chapters 7 and 8.)

   W. F. Allen says that different plantations have their
own peculiarities of Gullah speech. [119] There is extreme
simplification of both etymology and syntax. He discusses
other characteristics: the sounds of th and v, or f softened
into d and b; frequent interchange of v and w; clipping of
words and syllables; lengthening of short vowels; strange
words, corruptions of words, and words used in a peculiar
way; letters n, r, and y used euphonically; little inflection;
no distinction of gender, case, number, tense, or voice, and
little distinction in pronouns. The past tense of strong verbs
is used for the present and past time is expressed by been
or done. Auxiliaries are omitted and for is used as the sign
of the infinitive. The passive is rarely indicated.

   Marcellus S. Whaley says that there is no standard
Gullah. There is a recurrence of the sounds "uh," "e," "a,"
"ih," and "um," and a and an are seldom used as articles.
"The richness of the Gullah dialect is largely due to its var-
iableness; a variety in the shaded, the often unintentional, use
of several words for the same idea, depending upon the context, emphasis, voice inflection and fluency of the particular
speaker's style. It gives to the speech a picturesque sponta-
neity and easy euphony which lends itself so readily to rhythm." [120] Many words are run together. The accent is
placed on the last syllable of many words; k, g, t, and d are
left off at the end of a word and prefixes and suffixes are also omitted; the singular and plural are seldom differentiated,
and adjectives are used for both adjectives and adverbs.

Reed Smith emphasizes the idea that Gullah is a spoken, not a written speech, and the freedom from the restrictions of a written language has allowed the leveling and simplifying processes to have full sway. Since it was also first formulated as a medium of communication between master and slave, it was also a simplified form of English in phonology, grammar, and vocabulary, with elision, shortening, modification or difficult enunciation, and a minimum of forms for person, number, case, and tense. It is as nearly an uninflected tongue as it is possible to conceive. [121]

Hans Kurath says that the vocabulary is predominantly English and that about a dozen of the African words used by speakers of Gullah have acquired currency outside the present Gullah area, chiefly in the Lower South: buckra, "white man"; cooter, "box turtle"; goober, "peanut"; gumbo, "okra"; chigger, pinder, "peanut"; shout, "religious ring dance"; yam, "sweet potato." Kurath says that the structure of the subject phrase, the predicate phrase, and the sentence is essentially English and the only recurring syntactic feature that deviates from English is the equational sentence without the copula. [122]

Julia Peterkin says that the English vocabulary in Gullah is small but is used with economy and skill. "One gender serves for all three; singular and plural are disregarded along with tenses, while Gullah tongues wrap around words in a way that makes them unintelligible except to trained ears. Yet anyone familiar with the Gullah language finds the quaint dialect musical and charming and is constantly amused and delighted with the way these simple, untaught people contrive apt figures of speech to interpret subtle shades of meaning." [123]

Ivan Van Sertima lists the following characteristics of Gullah: [124] absence of gender distinction; absence of plural marker and possessive markers in nouns; no third person singular present tense marker; use of definite article mainly for specificity; frequent absence of the copula; no passive voice; words which resemble English words in sound but have different meanings in Gullah; use of double negative; placing of adjectives after the noun; use of same order in interrogative and declarative sentences; subject or object stated in Gullah, repeated by use of a personal pronoun, then statement made about the subject; word groups used for equivalent of a noun, verb, or adverb; use of habitual tense.

The Gullah Dialect in Literature

Edgar Allan Poe created a Negro character in "The Gold Bug" (1843) and provided him with a dialect. Caroline Gilman allowed some of her Negro characters to use Gullah in Recollections of a Southern Matron (1837). Joel Chandler Harris is credited with having Daddy Jack speak a few words of Gullah. But it is William Gilmore Simms who first used Gullah to any extent as a literary language.

Critics disagree as to Poe's use of dialect. Gonzales says that Poe "put into the mouth of a Charleston Negro such vocables as might have been used by a black sailor on an English ship a hundred years ago, or on the minstrel stage, but were never current on the South Carolina coast."[125] Killis Campbell says that he finds nothing particularly Charlestonian in the Negro's speech in "The Gold Bug." "The dialect, such as it is, doubtless is based on the speech of the darky slave as Poe knew him in Richmond and in Goochland County (at 'the Byrd')."[126] But Eric Stockton says that Poe invented no linguistic features for Jupiter, for they are all duplicable elsewhere. He concludes that Jupiter must stand or fall because of his dialect, which Stockton says is a quasi-Gullah, a literary convention based on the Negro speech of the southeastern coast with some Gullah features and the body of folk-speech that underlies all American dialects. "Jupiter talks something like Uncle Remus' Charleston and Savannah acquaintances."[127]

In 1833, almost a hundred years before Ambrose E. Gonzales published The Black Border (1922), with a glossary of Gullah words, William Gilmore SIMMS (1806-1870) published "A Scene of the Revolution" in The Book of My Lady (Philadelphia: Key and Riddle), pp. 259-276. Thus Simms is the first important American writer to use the Negro as a character in a short story and the first writer to allow the Negro character to speak the Gullah dialect.[128] "A study of Simms's use of Negro dialect shows that it is much less faulty than is generally thought. As a matter of fact, it is remarkably--almost scientifically--correct. The Gullah dialect in Simms's stories is not a haphazard attempt by a white man to reproduce the strange-sounding dialect of the Negro but is a consistent, unusually accurate reproduction of the actual sounds and words of the Carolina Gullah dialect, insofar as this peculiar dialect can ever be reproduced in print."[129] Both Gonzales and Simms wrote about the same

section of coastal Carolina, but Simms at this early period
was able to catch the sounds of the Gullah dialect accurately
and to reproduce them in writing "with an almost scientific
precision. " J. Allen Morris says that Simms must have
felt the necessity of making his Negro characters real and
thus allowed them to use their own speech.

> To do this satisfactorily, with no models to
> follow and no previous literary or scholarly work
> to assist him in his pioneer efforts, must have
> been a difficult task, for it required his reproduc-
> ing in print a dialect that to an uninitiated ear is
> almost hopelessly baffling and confusing.   Simms's
> ear, however, was well trained for his experiment.
> For years he had heard the Gullah dialect spoken;
> he had listened to it attentively, caught the sounds
> of individual words, and acquired a fairly large vo-
> cabulary of Gullah words.   To him these words had
> a positive literary value; they were to be used in
> his stories and novels. 130

Simms wrote four stories ("The Lazy Crow, " "Caloya, "
"The Snake of the Cabin, " and "The Bride of the Battle"),
all published before the Civil War, and at least nine novels,
in which Negroes are characters and in which the Gullah dialect is used. 131   The extent of Gullah ranges from four
words in Confession to seventy-seven pages in Woodcraft, or
a total of two hundred and twenty-five pages in nine novels.132
Morris analyzes Simms's Gullah words according to the laws
and analogies worked out by Reed Smith133 and concludes
that Simms was familiar with the fundamental principles gov-
erning such linguistic changes as consonant shifts, dropping
or slurring of letters, and aphaeresis, or the omission of a
letter, phoneme, or unstressed syllable at the beginning of
a word.   Morris points out some of the characteristics of
Simms's Gullah dialect and lists some examples of his use
of figurative language: "Ol' maussa hab de fire in he foot"
(gout).   "He git shet of dem'" (escaped).   "Dey mek trak'"
(ran).   "I terra [tell] um drip de hoe and pull foot dis way"
(hurry here).   "Dis nigger ain't able to lif' he body an' he
leg" (is tired).   "He hab he leg always" (holds his liquor
well).
    Nell Marie Nixon examined eight novels and three
stories of Simms as the basis for determining his use of
Gullah.   She says that Simms used dialect as one of his
major devices for it enabled him to individualize many of
his dialect speakers into satisfying literary characters. 134

Works:

Guy Rivers: A Tale of Georgia. New York: Harper and Brothers, 1834; rev. ed., New York: Redfield, 1855.

The Yemassee: A Romance of Carolina. 2 vols. New York: Harper and Brothers, 1835; rpt. New York: American Book Company, 1937, edited by Alexander Cowie.

The Partisan: A Tale of the Revolution. 2 vols. New York: Harper and Brothers, 1835; rev. ed., Chicago: Donohue, Hennsberry and Company, n.d.

Mellichampe: A Legend of the Santee. 2 vols. New York: Harper and Brothers, 1836; rev. ed., Chicago: Donohue, Hennsberry and Company, n.d.

The Sword and the Distaff, later published as Woodcraft. Charleston: Walker, Richards and Company, 1852; Philadelphia: Lippincott, Grembo and Company, 1853.

The Forayers. New York: Redfield, 1855; rev. ed., Chicago: Donohue, Hennsberry and Company, n.d.

Eutaw, 1856; rev. ed., Chicago: Donohue, Hennsberry and Company, n.d.

The Cassique of Kiawah. New York: Redfield, 1958.

"The Snake of the Cabin," "The Lazy Crow," and "Caloya" in The Wigwam and the Cabin. George Clark and Son, 1845; new rev. Chicago: Donohue, Hennsberry and Company, 1856; rpt. The Gregg Press, Inc., 1968.

The Centennial Edition of the Writings of William Gilmore Simms in 15 volumes is being published by the University of South Carolina Press. John C. Guilds is the general editor. Of the above works, the new edition will include The Wigwam and the Cabin, Guy Rivers, The Cassique of Kiawah, and The Yemassee.

Ambrose Elliott GONZALES (1857-1926) was born in Colleston County, South Carolina. He was the editor and owner of The State, a newspaper of Charleston, South Carolina, 1891-1926. He published four books on the lore and legends of the Gullah Negro.

Reed Smith says that Gonzales was peculiarly fitted to write Gullah. "He was nursed by a faithful Negro mauma; as a child was waited upon by and played with Negroes; he hunted and fished with them. These long and familiar relationships have given him a rarely comprehensive and sympathetic understanding of the Negro temperament, which to the value of his work as literature add the authenticity of history and sociology."[135] Mason Crum thinks that Gonzales was "able to portray the deep recesses of the Gullah Negro's mind in a manner unequaled by any of his contemporaries, and his ability to disclose the subtle wit and wisdom of the coastal Negro was most unusual. Unhappily, relatively few people will ever enjoy Gonzales's stories. They are so true to the life of the little-known people, and the dialect is so pure, that only those who have lived among the Gullahs can have a full appreciation of their meaning."[136]

Although he criticizes Gonzales for his racistic explanation of some of the structural characteristics of the Gullah dialect, William A. Stewart says that in spite of this "theoretical weakness," "Gonzales' literary rendition of Gullah was superb. Considering the accuracy of his dialect phonology and syntax, and the ease with which he handles subtle dialect differences and even individual switching behavior, he can certainly qualify as America's greatest dialect writer."[137]

John Bennett says of Gonzales: "As Gonzales writes Gullah it is a dialect alive, full of graphic humor, and vividly grotesque; stripped and divested of its interior freight of fun, I think the text upon the page would still be humorous; the very type would go pranking by like the crowds at Mardi Gras."[138]

Works:

The Black Border, Gullah Stories of the Carolina Coast. Columbia, S. C.: The State Company, 1922. 348 pp., 12 pages Foreword, 42 stories, Gullah Glossary, Appendix.

With Aesop Along the Black Border. Columbia, S. C.: The State Company, July, 1924. 298 pp., 60 fables, animal silhouettes by John Bennett; rpt. 1969, New York: Negro Universities Press. 198 pp., 6 pages Foreword, no illustrations.

The Captain, Stories of the Black Border. Columbia, S. C.: The State Company, October, 1924. 384 pp., 24 stories, 3 illustrations.

Laguerre, A Gascon of the Black Border. Columbia, S. C.: The State Company, December, 1924. 318 pp., 19 stories, 3 illustrations. Reprinted by Books for Libraries Press, Freeport, New York, 1972.

Short Selections:

"A Gullah's Tale of Woe," in The Black Border, pp. 283-241.

"A Riever of the Black Border," in The Captain. Reprinted in Stories of the South, Old and New. Edited by Addison Hibbard. Chapel Hill: University of North Carolina Press, 1931, pp. 309-321.

"Clever Alice," in Laguerre, A Gascon of the Black Border, pp. 53-69.

Julia PETERKIN (1880-1961) was born in Laurens County, South Carolina. She received two degrees from Converse College and taught school for several years before she married William George Peterkin and went to live on Lang Syne Plantation near Fort Motte, South Carolina, where she found the material for her fiction. She wrote three novels, forty-six stories and sketches, and Roll, Jordan, Roll (1933), a collection of non-fictional plantation sketches. She was awarded the Pulitzer Prize for Scarlet Sister Mary (1928). Her use of the Gullah dialect is praised by Donald Davidson, who says that her "first problem was to adapt this dialect to literary purposes, and her rendering, whether or not it is actually near to the Gullah talk itself, is unobtrusive and effective."139 She gives the essence of the dialect through a few basic Gullah words and the Gullah syntax and rhythms, but keeps close enough to regular English to be understood by the average reader.

Works:

Green Thursday. New York: The Bobbs-Merrill Company, 1924.

Black April. New York: The Bobbs-Merrill Company, 1927; rpt. Dunwoody, Georgia: Norman S. Berg, Publisher, 1972. 316 pp.

Scarlet Sister Mary. New York: The Bobbs-Merrill Company, 1928; rpt. Dunwoody, Georgia: Norman S. Berg, Publisher, n. d. 348 pp.

Bright Skin. New York: The Bobbs-Merrill Company, 1932; rpt. Dunwoody, Georgia: Norman S. Berg, Publisher, 1972. 348 pp.

Short Selections:

"Ashes," in Green Thursday. Also included in Collected Short Stories of Julia Peterkin. Selected and edited by Frank M. Durham. Columbia, S. C. : University of S. Carolina Press, 1970, pp. 143-154. In "Ashes," Peterkin has Maum Hannah use the Gullah dialect and the white man who builds the new house, Southern speech.

"Hunting 'Possums and Turkey," in Black April, pp. 129-137.

DuBose HEYWARD (1885-1940) was born in Charleston, South Carolina, into an impoverished Southern family. When he was twenty, he became a cotton checker and time-keeper for a steamship line on the Charleston waterfront. Here he was associated with the Negro stevedores who handled the cargo for the steamers that carried freight along the coast.
Heyward spoke the Gullah dialect but found it difficult to write so that it would be easily understood. In Porgy, his first novel, the Negro characters speak in a modified Gullah that is different from standard speech but is intelligible to the ordinary reader. In Mamba's Daughters and The Half Pint Flask, Gullah is treated in the same way, but in the dramatic version of Porgy only remnants of Gullah remain: "sentence structure as far as possible, the interchangeable sex pronouns, the pronunciation of otherwise familiar words like 'jedus,' and a few characteristic words like 'buckra' for 'white man' and 'shoutin'' for the typical bodily rhythm."140

Works:

Porgy. New York: George H. Doran Company, 1925; play version, with Dorothy Heyward, Garden City, N. Y. : Doubleday, Page, 1927.

<u>Mamba's Daughters</u>. Garden City, N. Y. : Doubleday and Company, 1929; play version, with Dorothy Heyward, New York: Farrar and Rinehart, 1929.

<u>The Half Pint Flask</u>. New York: Farrar and Rinehart, 1929. 55 pp. First published in <u>Bookman</u>, 1927; in The Best Short Stories of 1927. Edited by Edward J. O'Brien. New York: Dodd Mead and Company, 1928, pp. 142-157; and in <u>Stories of the South</u>. Edited by Addison Hibbard. Chapel Hill: University of North Carolina Press, 1931, pp. 341-360.

The Gullah Dialect in Literature: Folk Songs, Tales, and Sketches

William ELLIOTT (1787-1863) was born in Beaufort, South Carolina, into a prominent plantation family. He served in both houses of the state legislature and one term in the United States House of Representatives. He was an ardent hunter and fisherman. His story in Gullah dialect is "The Fire Hunter," in <u>Carolina Sports, by Land and Water</u>. Charleston, S. C. : Burgess and James, 1946. It is included in <u>Nineteenth Century Southern Fiction</u>. Edited by John Caldwell Guilds. Columbus, Ohio: Charles E. Merrill Publishing Company, 1970, pp. 167-173. 141

<u>Slave Songs of the United States</u>. New York: A. Simpson and Company, 1867; rtp. Peter Smith, 1951. 115 pp. Collected mainly at Port Royal, South Carolina, between 1861 and 1865, by officers of the Federal army and by mission teachers. A discussion of the Gullah dialect by William Francis and comments on the dialect and music by W. F. Allen, Charles Pickard Ware, and Lucy McKim Garrison are included. Allen (1830-1889) was born in Northboro, Massachusetts. He spent two years in the South with the Freedmen's and Sanitary Commissions at St. Helena Island, South Carolina, and at Helena, Arkansas.

Charles Colcock JONES, Jr. (1831-1893), of Savannah, Georgia, was a lawyer, historian, and writer. His collection of Negro myths is one of the early collections of stories in Gullah. Reed Smith says of his work: "Colonel Jones, a careful lawyer, handled the dialect correctly, and recorded with great exactness and without embellishment the stories as they were told him on the plantation. "[142] His collection is Negro Myths from the Georgia Coast, Told in the Vernacular. Boston: Houghton Mifflin Company, 1888; rpt. Detroit: Singing Tree Press, 1969. 116 pp., 5 pages of glossary.

Mrs. A. M. H. CHRISTENSEN, of Beaufort, South Carolina, recorded eighteen stories or fables which she had learned directly from the island Negroes, in the language of the story tellers of the Sea Islands. Some of her stories antedate those of Joel Chandler Harris. Mrs. Christensen states: "Two or three years before the advent of Uncle Remus, the writer had published a South-Carolina version of 'De Wolf, de Rabbit, an' de Tar Baby,' in the Springfield Republican, which was followed by several other similar tales in the New York Independent." (Afro-American Folk Lore, p. x). Her collection is Afro-American Folk Lore, Told Round Cabin Fires on the Sea Islands of South Carolina. First published in 1892 by the author; rpt. by Books for Libraries Press, 1971. 116 pp., 18 fables.

Elsie Clews PARSONS (1875-1941) published Folk-Tales of the Sea Islands, South Carolina. Memoirs of the American Folk-Lore Society, XVI (1923). Reprinted by the Folklore Association, Inc., 1968. 218 pp.

Marcellus S. WHALEY. The Old Types Pass, Gullah Sketches of the Carolina Sea Islands. Boston: The Christopher Publishing Company, 1925. 192 pp., 25 tales and sketches; glossary of 1500 words and 42 idioms; 5 songs with music; 8 illustrative sketches. A discussion (pp. 159-165) of the changes in pronunciation and the use of several words for the same idea shows the richness of the Gullah dialect. In the "Introduction," Whaley calls attention to the idea that the white children grew up with pickaninny companions and thus "the language and ideas of one to a certain extent became naturally engrafted upon the other. Many a white boy, upon going out into the world, had difficulty in lopping off the unnatural limbs of the dual development." Donnal, in "Buh Mink En Buh Roostuh," in The Old Types Pass, pp. 24-26, uses the same dialect as Dah Hero.

E. C. L. ADAMS (1876-   ), a white physician of Columbia, South Carolina, uses the dialect of the Negroes

of lower Richland County and of the great swamps of the
Congaree, a section of the heart of South Carolina and within a few miles of Columbia, in two collections of sketches.
Adams says that the dialect is English "shot through and influenced by the traditions and sentiments of the African
slaves. Very few genuine words are distinguishable but
there is a marked influence of the African sense of melody
and rhythm." He says that "this particular dialect, while
pure nigger, is neither the dialect of the coast nor of the
northern part of the Black Border, but is absolutely distinct, and is the product of soil, race, and environment.
In other words, it is English as adapted to the needs and
knowledge of these primitive peoples. Sometimes a word
that is pronounced correctly has several dialect meanings,
and several sounds of the same word may be found in a
single sentence. There is no rule."[143] But William A.
Stewart disagrees with Adams. He says: "Actually, the
many striking syntactic similarities between the two dialects
would suggest that the former is only a slightly de-creolized
form of the latter."[144] Adams's writings that use the Gullah dialect include:

Congaree Sketches, Scenes from Negro Life in the
Swamps of the Congaree and Tales Told by Tad and Scip of
Heaven and Other Miscellany. Introduction by Paul Green.
Chapel Hill: University of North Carolina Press, 1927. In-
cludes a "Word List" of 150 Congaree words, pp. 111-116.

Nigger to Nigger. New York: Charles Scribner's
Sons, 1928.

Short Selections: "The Hopkins Nigger," in Congaree
Sketches, pp. 2-4; "Old Brother Tries to Enter Heaven," in
Nigger to Nigger, pp. 213-217; "The Bear Fight," in Nigger
to Nigger, pp. 223-224.

Genevieve Wilcox CHANDLER was born in Marion,
South Carolina. She attended Flora MacDonald College, Red
Springs, North Carolina, and studied music and art in New
York City and in Liverpool, England. She spent some time
among the Negroes of the South Carolina coast. It is about
these that she writes in "A Gullah Story, De Flagg Storm,"
Americana No. 2. Recorded by Genevieve W. Chandler,
Murrells Inlet, South Carolina, in American Stuff. An An-
thology of Prose and Verse by Members of the Federal Writ-
ers' Project. Foreword by Henry G. Alsberg. New York:
The Viking Press, 1937, pp. 65-69.

John M. RHAME, "Flaming Youth," A Story in Gullah Dialect, American Speech (October, 1933), 39-43. "Notes on the Dialect" on page 43. Originally published in the State, Columbia, South Carolina.

Drums and Shadows. Survival Studies Among the Georgia Coastal Negroes. Savannah Unit Georgia Writers' Project, Works Projects Administration. Foreword by Guy B. Johnson. Photographs by Muriel and Malcolm Bell, Jr. Athens: University of Georgia Press, 1940; rpt. Spartanburg, S. C. : The Reprint Company, 1974. 274 pp. The material was collected by visits, interviews, and observations of the workers of the Georgia Writers' Project under the supervision of Mary Granger, with Georgia Coastal Negroes in twenty small communities, in an attempt to assess the African heritage of these people. Footnotes which give African parallels are used, and a glossary of Gullah words is included.

Gullah Dialect in Literature:
Additional Fictional Use of Gullah

In 1898, Elisabeth Carpenter SATTERTHWAIT published a novel in which the Negro characters speak Gullah, A Son of the Carolinas, A Story of the Hurricane upon the Sea Islands. Philadelphia: Henry Altemas; rpt. Books for Libraries Press, 1972. 273 pp.

Wilbur Daniel STEELE (1886-1970), a novelist, playwright, and author of several volumes of short stories, had his story "Conjuh" published in the Pictorial Review for 1929. It later appeared in The Best Short Stories of Wilbur Daniel Steele. Garden City, N. Y. : Doubleday and Company, 1946, pp. 316-335.

Chalmers S. MURRAY (1894-1975), Edisto Island correspondent for the Charleston News and Courier, wrote Here Come Joe Mungin, a novel concerned with the life of a sea island Gullah negro. Published by G. P. Putnam's Sons, 1942, 316 pp. , and reprinted by Bantam Books, 1954, this novel is considered to be the best modern use of Gullah in fiction. Rowena W. Tobias says of Murray's language: "an amazingly life-like Gullah speech is here without any use of complicated dialect" (Review of the novel in The News and Courier, February 15, 1942).

Records in the Gullah Dialect

Albert H. Stoddard. Animal Stories Told in the Gullah Dialect. Washington, D. C.: Library of Congress, Recording Laboratory. Edited by Duncan Emrich. Three longplaying records. Notes accompany the records.

Stoddard (1872-1954), of Savannah, Georgia, was born and brought up on Danfuski Island off the South Carolina coast. He grew up as a child with the Gullah Negroes and learned their speech and manner of telling the tales. He says: "As a result of schooling and communication with the outside world, the Gullah dialect has changed greatly, and one can no longer hear it as I learned it as a youngster. The only exception to this is to get the very older Negroes excited--they then occasionally lapse into the old Gullah." (From Recorded Interview at Library of Congress in 1949. Quoted on cover of record.)

Harold S. ("Dick") Reeves. Animal Tales in the Gullah Dialect told by Dick Reeves. n. d. One 7" reel. Library of Congress, Archive of Folk Song, No. 11402.

Harold S. Reeves and Russell Ward. One 10" reel. Gullah tales, Negro spirituals, and street cries from Charleston, S. C. n. d. From material loaned by Reeves and Wood. L. C. Archive of Folk Song, No. 11475.

Courtney Siceloff. One reel 10" tape of Gullah folk music and spirituals recorded by Courtney Siceloff on St. Helena Island, S. C. , prior to June 1955. L. C. Archive of Folk Song, No. 10899.

"It is impossible, furthermore, to have a complete understanding of any individual language without knowledge of its history. "

--Louis H. Gray. Foundations of Language. New York: Macmillan Company, 1939, p. 9.

LOUISIANA FRENCH CREOLE AND CAJUN DIALECTS

Historical Background

The Creoles are descendants of colonists who came to Louisiana from France and Spain before the time of the Louisiana Purchase and of Creoles from the West Indies. Supposedly, they constituted the aristocracy. Usually, they were city folks, landowners, and professional people. They occupied the lower part of Louisiana from Baton Rouge to the Gulf Coast. There were also small groups of French-speaking natives in eastern Missouri and in the area around Mobile, Alabama.[145] Creoles are predominantly French although there is a mixture of Spanish blood, but no true Creole ever had colored blood.[146]

The Cajuns are descendants of the French settlers whom the British expelled from Nova Scotia in the eighteenth century. They settled in various sections of Louisiana, but their main center is Attakapas. According to Thad St. Martin, the dividing line between the Acadian country and the Creole country is the Atchafalaya River.[147] The Acadians are primarily farmers, cattlemen, and fishermen. Their dialect shows the influence of their environment, but it is basically French. In many ways their language is not really a dialect but a literal translation from French. Sentences frequently end with an interrogative "Yes?" or "No?" Pronouns are scattered liberally, usually in the wrong places. When the Cajun cannot remember an English word or phrase, he uses a French one, falls back into English, and goes on from there.[148] The Cajun dialect is spoken in the Louisiana parishes of Acadia, Allen, Beauregard, Calcasien, Cameron, Evangeline, Iberia, Jefferson, David, Lafayette, St. Landry, St. Martin, and St. Mary, as well as a number of communities in other parishes.[149]

Studies of Louisiana French Creole and Cajun Dialects

1. Babington, Mima, and E. Bagby Atwood. Lexical Usage in Southern Louisiana. Publication of the Ameri-

can Dialect Society, Number 36 (November, 1961).   24 pp.
Twelve maps showing the locations of words are included.
          This study was begun by Mima Babington as the basis
of a doctoral dissertation at the University of Texas and was
completed by E. Bagby Atwood after her death in 1960.   The
study is primarily concerned with lexical usage in six Louisiana parishes centering around Bayou Lafourche, in the Acadian area, with limited observations of New Orleans usage
for comparison.   The parishes are Lafourche, Terrebonne,
St. Mary, St. James, Assumption, and Ascension.   The materials were collected by interviews with seventy inhabitants
of the area.   A questionnaire based on the work sheets for
the Linguistic Atlas and more directly based on the "Work
Sheets for Vocabulary Collection" was used.   The interviews
were conducted by Babington and her advanced students.   Information provided by the study leads to the following conclusions: a number of usages found in the area could not
have come from other areas; other usages that center in the
area extend also for distances beyond; there is a noticeable
resistance to the invasion of usages from other areas.   Thus
the French-speaking portion of Louisiana has made a major
contribution to the regional vocabulary of American English.

          2.   "The Creoles" and "The Cajuns" in Gumbo Ya-Ya,
A Collection of Louisiana Folk Tales.   Compiled by WPA,
Louisiana Writers' Project, with Lyle Saxon, State Director,
Edward Dreyer, Assistant State Director, and Robert Tallant,
Special Writer.   Boston: Houghton Mifflin Company, 1945,
pp. 138-206.
          An account of the history, social life, superstitions,
and language of the Creoles and Cajuns in Louisiana.

          3.   Fortier, Alcêe.   "The Acadians of Louisiana and
Their Dialect," PMLA, VI, No. 1 (1891), 64-94.
          A discussion in three parts.   Part I concerns the his-
tory of the Acadians in Nova Scotia and their expulsion by
the British and their arrival in Louisiana.   Part II describes
a visit to the Têche country and to St. Martinsville, the home
of several prominent Acadians, and to St. Mary's Parish,
where Fortier attended a local ball.   He then visited Côte
Blanche.   Part III is concerned with the Acadian dialects.
The dialects are different in each locality, a situation determined not only by the dialects of the early settlers but by
local influences.   Examples of the dialect from the Parish
of St. Martin and the Parish of St. Mary are given as well
as two letters which illustrate the dialect.   Characteristics
of the dialect include contractions, liaison of s and t, the

use of the pronoun of the first person singular with a plural verb, the dropping of the auxiliary être with reflexive verbs.

4. Kane, Harnett T. The Bayous of Louisiana. New York: William Morrow and Company, 1934, pp. 10-17.

Kane says that the first colonists to reach Louisiana at the close of the seventeenth century were men who came from France--military officers, merchants, and yeomen. Their children and their descendants became Creoles. The Acadians came a half century later and settled in the bayous where they have remained. Some of them even now do not speak English. The Acadian speech is a dialect or a set of dialects made up of terms common to French villages of the sixteenth century, of local peculiarities, of words that have taken on new meanings or forms and with sounds that have been transposed. "It is a kind of French with a Southern accent of its own, of variations within variations." The language differs from place to place and has borrowings from the English, the Spanish, the Indian, and the Negro. In addition, there are new words made up to describe new sights and sounds. Little attention is paid to gender and to distinguishing singulars and plurals.

5. Post, Lauren C. Cajun Sketches. From the Prairies of Southwest Louisiana. Baton Rouge: Louisiana State University Press, 1962. 215 pp.

A modification of a dissertation on "The Cultural Geography of the Prairies of Southwest Louisiana," based mainly on interviews with residents of the Cajun country. It concerns the everyday life of the modern Cajun.

6. Ramsey, Carolyn. Cajuns on the Bayous. New York: Hastings House, Publishers, 1957. 300 pp.

An account of the writer's search for the true Acadian, a search that led to her traveling and living with the people of the "Cajun Country" of Louisiana. The "Preface" gives an account of the Acadians and their life in Louisiana after their expulsion by the British from Nova Scotia in 1755.

7. St. Martin, Thad. "Cajuns," Yale Review, n. s., XXVI (Summer, 1937), 859-862.

The Creoles are descended from the colonists who came direct from France and Spain before the Louisiana Purchase and from the Creoles of the West Indies. The Acadians were the French whom the English expelled from Nova Scotia. In time, they, too, mixed with the Spanish in their region.

Thad St. Martin says that although they form two groups in Louisiana, the Creoles and the Acadians have, in general, the same racial heritage. The distinctions are in the circumstances in which they came to the state. But with modern education and present-day means of communication, both have lost their distinctiveness. Only in the remote country districts are they unchanged. 150

Louisiana French Creole and Cajun Dialects in Literature

George Washington CABLE (1844-1925) was born and brought up in New Orleans and knew first-hand the life he portrays in many of his stories and novels. "He knew the Creoles in the counting room, and he had Creole friends. He read and spoke French, and he studied the language and lore belonging to the various levels of French-speaking people, including the mulattoes and Negroes.... With his friend Lafcadio Hearn, ... he shared an interest in the racial mixture in the city, and together they studied, in whatever books were of any use and among the people themselves, their speech, their songs, and their traditions, whether of local or European or Caribbean of African origin.... The Creole patois interested him partly because it was almost unknown to linguists and printer's ink alike. "151 Richard Chase says of Cable: "He had a rich linguistic store to draw on and a highly developed ear for language, so that we hear at one time or another not only Creole English but Creole French and Negro French and English. The Creole English also varies according to the speaker. Most difficult of all are the few interpolated songs that combine French and the African dialects and whose rhythmic pattern and refrains seem to suggest New Orleans jazz. "152

Works:

Old Creole Days, 1879, contains six stories originally published in Scribner's Monthly and "Posson Jone," published in Appleton's Journal, 1876. Later editions include "Madame Delphine," published separately in 1881.

The Grandissimes, 1880, appeared serially in Scribner's Monthly beginning early in 1880. In the 1883 edition the dialect was simplified. Later printings are of this edition.

Bonaventure: A Prose Pastoral of Acadian Louisiana, 1888, is concerned with a Creole among Acadians. It contains "Carancro," "Grande Pointe," and "Au Large," all of which had appeared serially in the Century Magazine during 1887 and early 1888. Reprinted by Literature House, 1969.

Strange True Stories of Louisiana, 1889. Reprinted by Books for Libraries Press, 1970. 350 pp.

Strong Hearts, 1899. Three stories. Reprinted by Books for Libraries Press, 1970. 214 pp.

Creoles and Cajuns, Stories of Old Louisiana, 1899. A collection of stories from earlier publications. Reprinted, Gloucester, Mass.: Peter Smith, 1965. Edited by Arlin Turner.

Kate CHOPIN (1851-1904) was born in St. Louis, Missouri, the daughter of a Creole mother and an Irish father. She lived in St. Louis until her marriage to Oscar Chopin, the son of a French father and a Creole mother. They went to live in Louisiana, first in New Orleans and then on a plantation at Cloutiersville in Natchitoches Parish. Here she became acquainted with the Cane River Creoles, Cajuns, and Negroes. Natchitoches became her literary province.

Works:

At Fault, 1890. Concerned with Creole life in the Cane River section of central Louisiana.

Bayou Folk, 1894. Twenty-three stories and anecdotes of Louisiana. Reprinted by Gregg Press, Inc., 1967. 313 pp.

A Night in Acadie, 1897. A collection of stories.

The Complete Works of Kate Chopin. Edited and with an Introduction by Per Seyersted. Foreword by Edmund Wilson. Baton Rouge: Louisiana University Press, 1969. Two volumes. 1032 pp.

Grace Elizabeth KING (1852-1932) was born in New Orleans, Louisiana, and educated in the French schools of New Orleans. She began her writing career by contributing sketches of Creole life to the New Princeton Review.

Works:

Monsieur Motte, 1888. Reprinted by Books for Libraries Press, 1969. 327 pp.

Tales of Time and Place, 1888. Reprinted by AMS Press, Inc. , 1970. 303 pp.

Balcony Stories. The Century Company, 1892. Reprinted by Gregg Press, Inc. , 1968. Fourteen stories. 245 pp.

Lyle SAXON (1891-1946) was born in Baton Rouge, Louisiana. After graduating from Louisiana State University, he taught school for a year before he turned to newspaper work. He wrote many short stories as well as four nonfiction works dealing with the history and traditions of Louisiana.

Works:

"The Long Furrow, " Century Magazine, CXIV (October, 1927), 688-696.

Children of Strangers. Boston: Houghton Mifflin Company, 1937. 294 pp. Setting on Yucca plantation on Cane River in Louisiana. Four classes on Cane River are represented in the novel: the plantation owner and his family, the clerk or white "trash, " the mulattoes who look down on the black people, and the Negroes. The sermon at the backwoods Negro church on Easter morning is a real one that was taken down by the author.

Ada Jack CARVER (1892-   ) was born in Natchitoches, Louisiana, and until her marriage to John Snell, lived in that town. She attended Judson College and won a story prize while still an undergraduate. "Red Bone" won first prize in the Harper short-story contest in 1925, and her one-act play, "The Cajun, " won a prize in the Belasco Little Theatre Tournament in 1926.

Works:

Stories:

"Redbone," Harper's Magazine, CL (February, 1925), 257-270.

"Treeshy," Harper's Magazine, CLII (February, 1926), 353-365.

"The Old One," Harper's Magazine, CLIII (October, 1926), 545-554.

"Singing Woman," Harper's Magazine, CLIV (May, 1927), 689-695.

"Cotton Dolly," Harper's Magazine, CLVI (December, 1927), 32-41.

One-Act Play

"The Cajun," in The American Scene. Edited by Barrett Clark and Kenyon Nicholson. New York: D. Appleton and Company, 1930, pp. 501-516. Copyright, 1926, by Samuel French.

Records of Creole and Cajun Dialects

Anon. Cajun Songs from Louisiana. Phonodisc. New York: Folkways Records P438. 1956.

Anon. Creole Songs of Louisiana. Phonodisc. Folkways Records F A602.

Harry Oster (ed.). A Sample of Louisiana Folk Songs. Phonodisc. Louisiana Folklore Publication, No. 1. Includes Creole and Cajun songs; accompanied by a booklet of lyrics and explanatory notes.

"The land itself, the people who came to it, and their ways of exploiting it remain the leading factors that determine the distribution of the regional vocabulary."

    --E. Bagby Atwood. <u>The Regional Vocabulary of Texas</u>. Austin, Texas: <u>The University of Texas Press</u>, 1962, p. 23.

CHAPTER V

WESTERN DIALECTS

Historical Background

Although for studying the culture, the West may be
divided into the Upper Midwest, the Central Midwest, the
Rocky Mountain Region, the Mormon Region, the Interior
Southwest, the Pacific Southwest, and the Pacific Northwest,
as Raymond D. Gastil does, [153] the chief differences in the
language of the sections are in vocabulary and in the changes
caused by the various language groups encountered along the
borders and by foreign immigrant groups that settled in the
area. In general, the speech is that of the regions from
which the settlers came, modified by time and the ingenuity
of the settlers.

"... The speech of many Milwaukee, St. Louis, and
Cincinnati people of German ancestry, for example, is colored with the German dialect. Many residents of Holland,
Michigan, and the surrounding territory speak with Dutch
dialect variations. The speech of the people of Wyoming
has been influenced by the pioneer speech of Indian scouts,
trappers, miners, cowboys and cattlemen. Many inhabitants
of the mining districts of this state speak Middle Western,
but with traces of the Italian and Slav dialects. And certain
farming sections show definite Scandinavian speech influences.

"But, on the whole, the speech of most native-born
Americans is the Middle Western speech of Iowa, Kansas,
and Nebraska, with infiltrations from Missouri, Oklahoma,
and Texas in the border sections."[154]

Charlton Laird suggests following the westward movement of American English by tracing words belonging to dialects on the east coast. He says that the dialects of the
Midland and the North moved from the Atlantic coast on a
line roughly west from Pittsburgh across Ohio, Indiana, and
Illinois. North of this line are influences from New England

147

and New York.   South of this line the Midland is purer except when mountain Southern works north.   In addition, north
and south lines develop.   One line cuts through the Dakotas,
bringing farming terms from Iowa and Minnesota into contact
with mountain terms from Montana and Wyoming.   In Colorado, the dialects were established by two early gold rushes,
one bringing in Southernisms and one bringing in locutions
from North Midland. 155

        The far western movements followed two main lines:
one south of the Rocky Mountains and one up the Platte and
Missouri rivers.   The second movement divided, one following the Oregon Trail through Idaho down the Snake and Columbia rivers to Oregon and Washington, the other down the
Humbolt River to California.   On the west coast, some immigrants from the Northern speech areas arrived in ports
like San Francisco, and their dialects radiated from there.
A dialect associated with the Latter Day Saints spread from
the valley of the Great Salt Lake. 156

Studies in Western Dialect

        1.   Carmony, Martin.   "Aspects of Regional Speech
in Indiana, " in Studies in Linguistics in Honor of Raven I.
McDavid, Jr.   General Editor, Lawrence M. Davis.   University, Ala. :   University of Alabama Press, 1972.   pp. 9-
24.
        A survey of the studies of the Indiana dialect by Hans
Kurath (1928), Albert Marchwardt (1928, 1940, 1957), Raven
I. McDavid, Jr. (1956, 1958), Raven I. and Virginia McDavid
(1960).   McDavid divides the state into four major sections
on the basis of the parallels crossing it and determines the
Northern-North Midland boundary according to the use of
words for the bone from the chicken breast, the terms used
for the yard adjoining the barn, for snack, fishing worm,
salad (for edible tops of turnips), and weatherboarding.   An
analysis of a fragment of the Linguistic Atlas of the North
Central States (LANCS) materials on Indiana speech suggests
that in general the lexical data divides the state into three
principal dialect areas--Northern, North Midland, and South
Midland areas, with the South Midland area divided into two
parts.   The Western Indiana Regional Dialect Study (WIRDS)
has accumulated data on the nature and background of Indiana
speech.   One study is concerned with the vocabularies of
several hundred Indiana State University students.   The WIRDS
data suggest that there are at least six subareas not revealed
by the LANCS project.

2.   Haller, John M.   "Edward Eggleston, Linguist,"
Philological Quarterly, XXIV (October, 1945), 175-186.
     A survey of Eggleston's ideas and writings on lan-
guage and a discussion of the application of his ideas in his
novels.   Haller summarizes Eggleston's ideas about speech
under seven heads: the study of dialect and folk-speech is
a part of the social historian's task; language is not static
but is everchanging; language should be studied directly; folk-
speech is the most conservative part of language; language of
America has been affected little by the language of the Indians; American dialects are directly traceable to the dialects
of England at the time of colonial emigration; speech has its
individual aspects, both as to words and to individuals.   Haller concludes that although Eggleston was not a professional
philologist, he was a faithful recorder of the speech around
him, and he advocated the use and study of dialect at a time
when such views were not common.

3.   Harris, Jesse W.   "The Dialects of Appalachia
in Southern Illinois," American Speech, XXI (April, 1946),
96-99.
     Harris shows by a discussion of the vocabulary that
the dialect of Southern Illinois is a part of the dialect of
Appalachia since many of the pioneer inhabitants came directly from the Appalachian highlands of Virginia, Tennessee,
and the Carolinas and indirectly from Kentucky and inland
Tennessee.   Many of the locutions are still used by older
members of the section, but improved systems of education
and communication are causing many of the practices to dis-
appear.

4.   Hubbard, Claude.   "The Language of Ruxton's
Mountain Men," American Speech, XLIII (October, 1968),
216-221.
     In a fictionalized history of the trappers of the Rocky
Mountain region during four months of 1846 and 1847, George
Frederick Ruxton attempts to reproduce the actual speech of
the mountain men--their vocabulary, some of their syntax,
and the peculiarities of their pronunciation.   Hubbard says
that since the nonstandard English of the trappers contains
the features common to nonstandard speech across the country, its distinctiveness is found almost entirely in the vocabulary, which, he says, shows the influence of contacts with
the Indians and includes words adopted from French and
Spanish.   Ruxton's accuracy of observation is shown in the
extent to which the vocabulary he attributed to the mountain
men has been verified by M. M. Mathews in A Dictionary
of Americanisms, 1951.

5.   McDavid, Raven I., Jr., and Virginia G. McDavid. "Grammatical Differences in the North Central States," American Speech, XXXV (February, 1960), 5-19.

A summary of grammatical evidence in the field records for the Linguistic Atlas of the North Central States to determine whether the regional dialect differences, established for the Atlantic seaboard, continue inland, to discover whether secondary settlement areas also show regional differences in grammar, to learn what the grammatical practices are that actually differentiate cultivated from uncultivated usage so that English teachers may work on practices that may stigmatize their students.   Modifications of the principles of American linguistic geography necessary for the situation in the North Central States include: a network of from twenty-five to forty communities to provide adequate coverage for a survey of an area of secondary settlement; informants native to their communities, representing at least two different groups in each community by age, education, and ethnic origin; a questionnaire containing items from the daily experience of most informants and designed to reveal regional and social differences in vocabulary, pronunciation, and grammar; field investigators with intensive training including experienced workers; impressionistic transcription on the spot in a finely graded phonetic alphabet.   The writers conclude on the basis of their evidence that regional differences in grammar are less sharp in the North Central States than along the Atlantic seaboard, although many regional differences can be observed in every level of usage; the regionally distinctive grammatical forms in the North Central States reflect the usage of the Northern and South Midland regions of the Atlantic seaboard; arteries of communication have facilitated the spread of Northern and South Midland forms; the more spectacular relic forms are rare; the social differences in the speech of the North Central region are not reflected in the judgments of usage made by those who prepare teaching materials.

6.   Pederson, Lee A.   The Pronunciation of English in Metropolitan Chicago.   Publications of the American Dialect Society, Number 44 (November, 1965).   87 pp.

This study is "an attempt to relate the speech of the rural and suburban satellites to the dialect of the urban center, to identify the speech characteristics of the social groups within this speech community, and to provide inventorial data for future research into the relationships of language and culture in Metropolitan Chicago."   Chapter I describes the preliminary procedures (area delimitation, selection and classification of informants, interviews).   Chapter II is an analysis of the fifty-five primary informants and eighty-one subsidiary informants. The third chapter presents the findings of the study and makes recommendations as to the kinds of investigation that would be useful to complete the description of Chicago speech as outlined in the report.

7. Reed, Carroll E. "The Pronunciation of English in the Pacific Northwest," in Readings in American Dialectology. Edited by Harold B. Allen and Gary N. Underwood. New York: Appleton-Century-Crofts, 1971, pp. 115-121. Reprinted from Language, XXXVII (1961), 559-564.
An investigation into the elements of phonemic structure and the distribution of phonetic data with regard to Northwest pronunciation as a reflection of eastern variants in Washington, Idaho, and adjacent sections of Oregon and Montana. The study shows the residual effects of Northern and North Midland speech forms in the Pacific Northwest, particularly with regard to the elements of phonemic structure.

8. Reed, David W. "Eastern Dialect Words in California," in Readings in American Dialectology. Edited by Harold B. Allen and Gary N. Underwood. New York: Appleton-Century-Crofts, 1971, pp. 105-114. Reprinted from Publications of American Dialect Society, XXI (1954), 3-15.
A study to determine the relation of language forms in California with widespread distributions in the East, and the relation of the settlement history to the origin of local variants. Evidence shows that the popularity of a word in California tends to reflect its use in Eastern dialects. Words that occur in parts of two major areas or exclusively in a single major area tend to be in minority usage or non-existent in California. Such words are usually Northern, Midland, or partly both in the Atlantic Coast states and are moderately frequent in the Great Lakes region.

9. Sawyer, Janet B. "Aloofness from Spanish Influence in Texas English," Word, XV (1959), 270-281.
Contrary to the usual effect of immigrant language on the native language, that of being submerged after a few generations, no substratum formation of the Spanish language on the English language in San Antonio, Texas, could be found by Sawyer in her dialect study of San Antonio, Texas. For the study, seven native speakers of English and seven native speakers of Spanish were interviewed. All were permanent residents of the second generation, varying in age, education, and economic status. Sawyer concludes that linguistic evidence

reveals that the English in San Antonio has not been affected by Spanish in phonology, morphology, or syntax, and that she found no evidence that Spanish contact is responsible for additions to the lexicon of San Antonio English.

Western Dialects in Literature

George Frederick RUXTON (1821-1848) was born in England. He went to Sandhurst but was expelled for rebellion against the rules. He fought in the Civil War in Spain, enlisted in the British Army and was sent to Canada. He sold his lieutenant's commission and went deep into the forests of Upper Canada. After a visit to England, he went to Africa. At the outbreak of the Mexican War, he went to Mexico and then northward to El Paso and Sante Fé. He spent most of the winter and spring of 1847 at a traders' fort on the present site of Pueblo, Colorado. Life in the Far West is a narrative of the adventures of his trapper companions of the Far West. It ran serially in Blackwood's Edinburgh Magazine, June to November, 1848.

Works:

Life in the Far West. Edited by Leroy R. Hafen, with a Foreword by Mae Reed Porter. Norman, Okla. : University of Oklahoma Press, 1951. 252 pp. Original English editions of 1848, 1850, 1851, 1861, and 1867; American editions in 1849, 1855, 1859, and 1915; German edition in 1852.

Bret HARTE (1836-1902) was born in Albany, New York, but was taken West as a young boy, arriving in Oakland, California, at the age of seventeen. He had a Jewish grandfather, a Catholic father, and an Episcopalian mother. He worked as a drug clerk and an express messenger, taught school, mined for gold. He became a job printer and an assistant editor of the North Californian at Uniontown. In 1860 he returned to San Francisco and wrote for The Golden Era and The Californian. He became editor of the Overland Monthly when it was founded in 1868. In this journal he published the writings that established his reputation. Although Harte's dialect has been criticized as being Harte's own creation rather than a transcript of speech actually used at that time, C. Alphonso Smith says that of "Bret Harte's three hundred dialect words and phrases a mere handful remain unidentified as American. "[157]

Works:

Tennessee's Partner, 1870.

How Santa Claus Came to Simpson's Bar, 1873.

John HAY (1836-1905) was born in Salem, Indiana. He graduated from Brown University, became a student of law, and later an assistant private secretary to Lincoln. He served as ambassador to Great Britain and as Secretary of State under both McKinley and Theodore Roosevelt. He became famous for his ballads of the Pikes. "A 'Pike,'" says Bayard Taylor, "in the California dialect, is a native of Missouri, Arkansas, Northern Texas or Southern Illinois. The first emigrants that came over the plains were from Pike County, Missouri; but as the phrase, 'a Pike County man,' was altogether too long for this short life of ours, it was soon abbreviated into 'a Pike.' Besides, the emigrants from the aforementioned localities belonged evidently to the same genus, and the epithet 'Western' was by no means sufficiently descriptive. The New England type is reproduced in Michigan and Wisconsin; the New York, in northern Illinois; the Pennsylvanian, in Ohio; the Virginian, in Kentucky; but the Pike is a creature different from these. He is the Anglo-Saxon relapsed into semibarbarism. He is long, lathy and sallow; he expectorates vehemently; he takes naturally to whiskey ... he has little respect for the rights of others; he distrusts men in 'store-clothes,' but venerates the memory of Andrew Jackson; finally, he has an implacable dislike to trees."[158] George Philip Krapp says of Hay's "Little Breeches": "But when one looks more closely at the local dialect words in this poem one finds few of them that may be regarded as peculiar to a Southwestern or Pike County dialect.... The so-called Southwestern dialect as it has existed in literature has been in reality merely low colloquial speech with an addition of certain details from New England and from Southern dialect speech."[159]

Works:

Pike County Ballads, 1971. Six short narrative poems in the "Pike" dialect.

Edward EGGLESTON (1837-1902) was born in Vevay, Indiana, a village on the Ohio River. In 1871, he became

editor of Hearth and Home, and from 1874 to 1879 he preach-
ed in the Church of Christian Endeavor which he founded in
Brooklyn. In 1879, he resigned to earn his living as a writer. He wrote history as well as fiction. John M. Haller
says of Eggleston: "Although not a professional philologist,
he became a faithful recorder of the speech which he heard
around him, a crusader for the extended use and study of
dialect, and a holder of advanced linguistic views in a day
when to hold such views was a rarity and a distinction. "[160]

Works:

The Hoosier School-Master, 1871. The Revised Edition, 1892, contains an Introduction and Notes on the Dialect
by the Author, with Character Sketches by F. Opper and
Other Illustrations by W. E. B. Starkweather. 281 pp.

The End of the World, 1872.

Roxy, 1878. Reprinted by The Gregg Press, Inc.,
1968. 432 pp.

The Graysons, 1888.

James Whitcomb RILEY (1849-1916) was a native of
Greenfield, Indiana. His father was a lawyer in comfortable
circumstances. Riley studied law but left it to join a traveling troupe of actors who sold patent medicine during inter-
missions. He settled in Indianapolis and while on the staff
of the Indianapolis Journal began printing dialect poems.
The first collection of his poems appeared in 1883. Clara
E. Laughlin says of Riley: "For his dialect poetry he kept
notebooks as accurate as a scientist's. Not only was the
euphony of the dialectics a careful study with him, but he
knew why some children, for instance, say 'thist,' instead
of 'just,' and why others say 'ist.' There was nothing haphazard in any of his work. The philologist of the future,
studying Middle Western colloquialisms of the late nineteenth
century, may depend on Riley's transcription of them as the
most exact ever made. "[161] (For an analysis of Riley's dialect, see Randall, p. 25.)

Works:

The Ole Swimmin' Hole, 1883.

Afterwhiles, 1887.

Rhymes of Childhood, 1890.

Farm-Rhymes, 1901.

Neighborly Poems and Dialect Sketches. New York:
Charles Scribner's Sons, 1917. 203 pp. Volume I of Home-
stead Edition. Includes "An Old Settler's Story," pp. 133-
184, in dialect, and "Dialect in Literature," pp. 187-203,
originally published in The Forum, XIV (December, 1892),
465-473.

Alfred Henry LEWIS (1858-1914) was a lawyer who
went West with his family in the early eighteen eighties.
He became a newspaper man. He wrote fictionized biographies, novels of political life, and stories of the New York
underworld, but his most popular works are the six volumes
of the Wolfville books, dialect tales of the mining and cattle-
raising frontier.

Works:

Wolfville. New York: J. B. Lippincott, 1897.

Hamlin GARLAND (1860-1940) was born on a farm in
western Wisconsin. He moved with his family to northeastern Iowa and then to northeastern South Dakota. Between
1884 and 1887 he studied in Boston. He returned to South
Dakota in 1887 to visit his family and was shocked by the
ugliness of the life there. He returned to Boston and wrote
Main-Travelled Roads. He wrote sixteen novels between
1895 and 1916. He moved to New York in 1916 and began
to write his autobiography. A Daughter of the Middle Border
won the Pulitzer Prize for biography in 1922. In "The Local
Novel," in Crumbling Idols, 1903, Garland says:
"Both drama and novel will be colloquial. This does
not mean that they will be exclusively in the dialects, but
the actual speech of the people of each locality will unques-
tionably be studied more closely than ever before. Dialect
is the life of a language, precisely as the common people of
the nation form the sustaining power of its social life and
art."162

Works:

Main-Travelled Roads, 1891. Contains eleven stories including "Under the Lion's Paw," 1889, and "Mrs. Ripley's Trip," first published in Harper's Weekly, November 24, 1888.

Prairie Folks, 1893, 1899. Reprinted by AMS Press, 1969. 284 pp. Verse and prose.

Ring W. LARDNER (1885-1933) was born in Niles, Michigan. He attended Armour Institute in Chicago for a semester, did odd jobs, and began a career in journalism. Later he became sports writer for the Chicago Examiner.

Works:

You Know Me, Al, 1916.

How to Write Short Stories. New York: Charles Scribner's Sons, 1924, 1950. Contains ten stories including "The Golden Honeymoon."

Round Up. New York: Charles Scribner's Sons, 1929. 467 pp. Contains thirty-five stories.

Harvey FERGUSSON (1890-1971) was born in Albuquerque, New Mexico. He graduated from Washington and Lee University in 1911. He lived in Washington, D. C. and New York before going to California. He is the author of ten novels and three books of nonfiction.

Works:

The Blood of the Conquerors, 1921.

Wolf Song. New York: Alfred A. Knopf, 1927.

Oliver LA FARGE (1901-   ) was born in New York City and educated at Harvard. He went to the Southwest because of his interest in anthropology. After teaching for two years at Tulane University and two years with the Army Air Force, he has devoted his time to writing.

Works:

Laughing Boy.   Boston: Houghton Mifflin Company,
1929.   302 pp.

The Enemy Gods.   Boston: Houghton Mifflin Company,
1937.   325 pp.

John STEINBECK (1902-1965), a native of Salinas,
California, attended Stanford University for four years as a
special student in marine biology.   After leaving Stanford,
he worked briefly as a reporter in New York City but returned to California because of illness.   He was awarded
the Pulitzer Prize for Grapes of Wrath.   1940, and the Nobel
Prize for Literature in 1962.

Works:

The Grapes of Wrath, 1939.

The Pastures of Heaven, 1932.   Short stories.

The Long Valley, 1938.   Short stories.

George Sessions PERRY (1910-1956) was born in
Rockdale, Texas.   He attended Southwestern University at
Georgetown, Texas, Purdue, and the University of Houston,
but did not complete the freshman year.   From 1942 to 1945,
he was a Correspondent with the Army Air Forces in Italy.
He has written stories for the Saturday Evening Post and for
other magazines.

Works:

Walls Rise Up, 1939.

Hold Autumn in Your Hand.   New York: Viking Press,
1941.

Hackberry Cavalier.   New York: Viking Press, 1944.
246 pp.   Seventeen short stories.

Records in Western Dialect

An Informal Hour with J. Frank Dobie. One 12" record in Texas accent. Spoken Arts. Includes "Trail-Drivers' Song" and "The Mezcla Man."

"But the masters of literary prose have seldom left their territorial and cultural frontiers. There is no such thing as the international novel or international drama. Literature is by its very nature bound to a people, a region, a language, even a dialect."

--Isaac Bashevis Singer, Book World, 1968. Quoted in Black Voices. Edited by Abraham Chapman. Mentor Edition. New York and London: The New American Library, 1968, p. 38.

CHAPTER VI

DIALECTS USED BY WRITERS OF ENGLISH
AS A SECOND LANGUAGE

Studies of the Dialects

1. Brody, Alter. "Yiddish in American Fiction," American Mercury, VII (February, 1926), 205-207.
References to the dialect of "Yidgin English" as used by such writers as Anzia Yezierska, Myra Kelly, David Freidman, Bruno Lessing, Fannie Hurst, and Israel Zangwill. Brody says that Yiddish is too rich a language to be exploited superficially. It is, he says, an autonomous language, a Middle German dialect which the German Jews adapted in the Middle Ages, with its own peculiar rhythms and imagery.

2. Feinsilver, Lillian Mermin. "Yiddish and American English," in The Golden Land. Edited by Azriel Eisenberg. New York: Thomas Yoseloff, 1964, pp. 483-491. Reprinted from The Chicago Jewish Forum, XVIII.
A discussion of Yiddish influence on American English: Yiddish words that are used outright, translated Yiddish expressions, expressions that are "flavored" by the Yiddish language, the Yiddish effect of "speech melody," the hybrid adoption of English by Yiddish, and changes in syntax or meaning by the adopted words.

3. Feinsilver, Lillian Mermin. "Yiddish Idioms in American English," American Speech, XXXVII (February-December, 1962), 200-206.
A further discussion of words and expressions from Yiddish that have become a part of American English through loan words, through translation, or through word-play.

4. Glissmeyer, Gloria. "Some Characteristics of English in Hawaii," in Varieties of Present-Day English. Edited by Richard W. Bailey and Jay L. Robinson. New York: Macmillan Company, 1973, pp. 190-222.

Glissmeyer gives the highlights of the language of Hawaii as presented by John E. Reinecke, Language and Dialect in Hawaii, edited by Stanley M. Tsusaki, 1969, a list of the research that has been done on English dialects in Hawaii, a discussion of the phonology of the region known as Keaukaha studied by Glissmeyer, and the lexicon and syntax of Hawaii English. She says that Hawaii English is a recent member of the world's English dialect systems, and that it seems premature at the present time to generalize about the dialect from the limited data available. She says, however, that extended linguistic studies of the dialects in Hawaii should add to our understanding of language variation throughout the world since Japanese, Chinese, some of the Philippine languages, and possibly Hawaiian as well as English can now be observed in the actual process of change.

5. Leechman, Douglas, and Robert A. Hall. "American Indian Pidgin English: Attestations and Grammatical Peculiarities," American Speech, XXX (February-December, 1955), 163-171.

This article presents and analyzes material on American Indian Pidgin English with the idea of obtaining information on the linguistic culture of the Indian and of aiding the historical study of pidgin English. Thirty-eight passages, ranging in time from 1641 to 1946, collected by Leechman, are analyzed by Hall for their linguistic aspects and from which an outline of the linguistic structure of AIPE is drawn. The authors conclude that AIPE presents basically the same characteristics of reduction and restructuring as do the other varieties of pidgin English.

6. Miller, Mary Rita. "Attestations of American Indian Pidgin English in Fiction and Nonfiction," American Speech, XLII (May, 1967), 142-147.

The confinement of Indians to reservations and to separate schools did not allow the Indians and Europeans to learn each other's languages in the Northwest. Now, however, the picture is changing and many of the Indians are giving up their tribal language in favor of a type of English. Examples of American Indian Pidgin English are still few but examples may be found in fiction as well as in nonfiction. The characteristics of the language include: the lack of an equational verb; lack of tense, person markers, auxiliaries, and modals; been as a past tense marker without an accompanying verb; personal pronouns different from standard English usage; um and him as determiners; complements and objects often omitted; absence of prepositions; tendency to repeat the noun subject; subjects often omitted; use of for to express purpose; few articles and plurals; no for negation; [r] and [l] often confused; th for d.

7. Reinecke, John E. Language and Dialect in Hawaii. A Sociolinguistic History to 1935. Edited by Stanley M. Tsuzaki. Honolulu: University of Hawaii Press, 1968. 254 pp. An Appendix gives "Examples of Makeshift and Dialectal English Used in the Hawaiian Islands." A bibliography of 27 pages follows.

A minimally revised version of an M.A. thesis written at the University of Hawaii in 1935.

8. Thomas, C. K. "Jewish Dialect and New York Dialect," American Speech, VII (June, 1932), 321-326.

A study of the speech of 112 students of Cornell University divided into three groups: Jews (75) from New York City and its suburbs, Gentiles (19) from the same area, Jews (18) who had lived all of their lives at a distance from New York City. Thomas concludes tentatively from the study that a good bit of what passes for Jewish dialect is really New York dialect, and that many of the errors he found also occur in Gentile speech.

9. Wolfe, George. "Notes on American Yiddish," American Mercury, XXIX, No. 116 (August, 1933), 473-479.

The article is divided into four parts. Part I concerns the development of American Yiddish, which Wolfe says is an almost unexplored field by the student of American speech. Part II deals with the infiltration of English loan-words into Yiddish. Part III concerns linguistic borrowings in informal conversation. Part IV discusses the attitudes of Yiddish writers toward English borrowings.

Writers of English as a Second Language

Thomas Augustine DALY (1871-1948) was born in Philadelphia. He attended Villanova College and Fordham University, but quit at the end of his sophomore year to become a newspaper man. He is best known for his interpretations of Irish and Italian immigrants.

Works:

Canzoni, 1906.

<u>Carmina</u>, 1909.

<u>Selected Poems of T. A. Daly</u>. New York: Harcourt,
Brace, 1936.

Sidney HOWARD (1891-1939) was born in Oakland,
California. After graduating from the University of California in 1915, he spent a year in Switzerland. In 1916, he
joined George Pierce Baker's 47 Workshop at Harvard, but
left to serve as an ambulance driver in World War I. Later
he joined the American Air Force in France. In addition to
writing over twenty plays, he wrote a book of short stories
and numerous newspaper articles. <u>They Knew What They</u>
<u>Wanted</u> won the Pulitzer Prize for drama for 1924. The
scene of the play is the home of an Italian winegrower in
the Napa Valley of California.

Works:

<u>They Knew What They Wanted</u>, 1924, in <u>Twenty-Five</u>
<u>Best Plays of the American Theatre</u>. Early Series. Edited
and with an Introduction by John Gassner. New York:
Crown Publishers, 1949, pp. 91-122.

Guido D'AGOSTINO (1906-   ) was born in New York
City, the son of Italian immigrant parents. During World
War II he served with the Office of War Information in Italy.
He wrote "The Dream of Angelo Zara" as a propaganda piece
for broadcasting to the enemy. Rewritten as a short story,
it was published in <u>Story</u>, 1942. Guido D'Agostino also wrote
two novels.

Works:

"The Dream of Angelo Zara," in <u>As I Pass, O Man-</u>
<u>hattan</u>. <u>An Anthology of Life in New York</u>. Edited by Esther
Morgan McCullough. North Bennington, Vt.: Coley Taylor,
Inc., Publishers, 1956, pp. 575-582.

<u>Olives on the Apple Tree</u>, 1940.

<u>Hills Beyond Manhattan</u>, 1947.

Leo C. ROSTEN (1908-   ) was born in Poland but
has spent most of his life in America. A political scientist,

teacher, research worker, editor, and humorist, he has made various contributions to American life. His dialect stories, written under the pseudonym of Leonard Q. Ross, first appeared in The New Yorker. These stories recount the Americanization of Mr. Hyman Kaplan and other immigrants in attendance at the American Night Preparatory School for Adults. These stories show some of the difficulties encountered by foreigners learning English. In the "Preface" to The Return, Rosten tells how he came to write the stories of Mr. Hyman Kaplan and comments on the difficulty in writing dialect and especially in having characters speak as well as write dialect. "There is a magic in dialect," he says, "which can liberate us from the prison of the familiar."

Works:

The Education of H*Y*M*A*N K*A*P*L*A*N. New York: Harcourt, Brace and Company, 1932.

The Return of H*Y*M*A*N K*A*P*L*A*N. New York: Harper and Row, Publishers, 1938, 1959.

Bernard MALAMUD (1914-   ) was born in Brooklyn, New York. He received the B.A. degree from the College of the City of New York in 1936 and became an English teacher in the evening high schools of New York City while studying for an M.A. degree at Columbia University. He taught at Oregon State College in Corvallis and in 1961 joined the staff of Bennington College, in Vermont. His writings include collections of short stories, novels, and a partly autobiographical work. In commenting on the language of "Take Pity," from The Magic Barrel, Alfred Kazin says: "There is a Doomsday terseness to Jewish speech--as if the book of life were about to close shut with a bang. Malamud had caught this quality with an intimacy of understanding that is utterly remarkable."163

Works:

The Magic Barrel. New York: Farrar, Straus and Giroux, Inc., 1958.

Idiots First, 1963. Includes "The Jewbird," which was first published in The Reporter, April 11, 1963.

Amado MURO, a first-generation Mexican American, was born in Parral, Chihuahua, Mexico, in 1931. He came to El Paso, Texas, at the age of nine and has lived there most of his life. Here he has worked at a number of jobs and has used writing stories and sketches as his vocation. His work has appeared in the Arizona Quarterly, New Mexico Review, and The Texas Observer.

Works:

"Mala Torres" and "María Tepache," in The Chicanos. Mexican American Voices. Edited by Ed Ludwig and James Santibañez. Baltimore, Md.: Penguin Books, Inc., pp. 37-42 and pp. 127-131. Reprinted from the Arizona Quarterly (Summer, 1968).

Records by Writers of English as a Second Language

The Education and Return of Hyman Kaplan. Read by Leo Rosten. Includes "Christopher Kaplan," "The Distressing Dream of Mr. Parkhill," "Mr. Kaplan and Shakespeare," and "Mr. Kaplan and the Magi." Spoken Arts, No. 950.

NOTES

PREFACE

1. Raven I. McDavid, Jr. "Dialect Geography and Social Science Problems," Social Forces, XXV (December, 1946), 168.
2. American Renaissance. New York: Oxford University Press, 1941, p. xv.

CHAPTER I: American English Dialects

3. A History of the English Language. New York: Appleton-Century-Crofts, Inc. , Second Edition, 1957, pp. 439-442.
4. American English. New York: Oxford University Press, 1958, pp. 135-136.
5. A Word Geography of the Eastern United States. Ann Arbor: University of Michigan Press, 1949, Figure 3.
6. Language and Languages. San Francisco: Chandler Publishing Company, 1972, p. 17.
7. An Introduction to the Phonetics of American English. New York: The Ronald Press Company, Second Edition, 1958, Figure 4.
8. The Pronunciation of American English: An Introduction to Phonetics. New York: Appleton-Century-Crofts, Inc. , 1960, pp. 45, 51.
9. "Literary Dialects," in The English Language in America. New York: The Century Company, 1925, I, 230-231.
10. English Dialects. New York: Oxford University Press, 1963, p. 13.
11. "Dialect," in Encyclopedia of the Social Sciences. New York: Macmillan Company, 1931, V, 123.
12. "Sense and Nonsense About American Dialects," PMLA, LXXXI (May, 1966), 10.

13. "Dialects: British and American Standard and Nonstandard," in Linguistics Today. Edited by Archibald Hill. New York and London: Basic Books, Inc., 1969, p. 80.

14. Trager, p. 16.

15. Brook, p. 205.

16. "Use of Field Materials in the Determination of Dialect Groupings," The Quarterly Journal of Speech, XLI (December, 1955), 364-365.

17. "Needed Research in Southern Dialects," in Perspectives on the South: Agenda for Research. Edited by Edgar T. Thompson. Durham, N.C.: Duke University Press, 1967, p. 123.

18. Raven I. McDavid, Jr., and Virginia G. McDavid. "Grammatical Differences in the North Central States," American Speech, XXXV (1960), 17, footnote 21.

19. "American English Dialects," in W. Nelson Francis. The Structure of American English. New York: The Ronald Press Company, 1958, pp. 483-485.

20. Arthur J. Bronstein. The Pronunciation of American English. An Introduction to Phonetics. New York: Appleton-Century-Crofts, Inc., 1960, pp. 42-43.

21. Language in America. New York and Cleveland: The World Publishing Company, 1970, pp. 154-155. See also Map 5, pp. 156-157.

22. "Geography and the American Language: An Approach to Literacy," in Language and Learning. Edited by Janet A. Emig, James T. Fleming, Helen M. Popp. New York: Harcourt, Brace and World, Inc., 1966, p. 150.

23. "Variations in Standard American English," Elementary English, XLV (May, 1968), 561-562.

24. "Introduction," Biglow Papers. Second Series. Elmwood Edition. New York: AMS Press, Inc., 1966, pp. 5-79.

25. Extraterritorial. New York: Atheneum Publishers, 1971, p. 150.

26. "The Novelist's Use of Dialect," The Writer, XLVII (January, 1935), 40.

27. "The Psychology of Dialect Writing," The Bookman, XLIII (July, 1926), 524.

28. "Preface: The Confessions of Mr. Parkhill," in The Return of H*Y*M*A*N K*A*P*L*A*N. New York: Harper and Brothers, 1938, p. 14.

29. "Introduction," Uncle Remus: His Songs and Sayings. New York and London: D. Appleton and Company, 1930. New and revised edition, p. viii. The first edition was published in 1880.

30. "A Theory of Literary Dialects," Tulane Studies in English, II (1950), 181-182.

CHAPTER II: New England Dialects

31. Ann Arbor: The University of Michigan Press, 1949, Chapter II.
32. Hans Kurath. Handbook of the Linguistic Geography of New England. Providence, R.I.: Brown University, 1939, pp. 1-25.
33. Dialects of American English. Cleveland and New York: The World Publishing Company, 1967, p. 22.
34. Ibid., p. 17.
35. Raymond D. Gastil. Cultural Regions of the United States. Seattle, Washington: University of Washington Press, 1975, p. 80.
36. Ibid.
37. Hans Kurath. Studies in Area Linguistics. Bloomington, Indiana: Indiana University Press, 1972, p. 45.
38. "Editor's Drawer," Harper's Magazine, IV (April, 1852), 705.
39. "Preface," Oldtown Folks. Boston: Fields, Osgood & Company, 1869, pp. iii-iv.
40. "Preface" to The Best Short Stories of Sarah Orne Jewett. Mayflower Edition. Boston: Houghton Mifflin Company, 1925, in Willa Cather on Writing. With a Foreword by Stephen Tennant. New York: Alfred A. Knopf, 1936, pp. 56-57.

CHAPTER III: The Middle Atlantic Dialects

41. C. F. Thomas. An Introduction to the Phonetics of American English. Second Edition. New York: Ronald Press, 1958, p. 222. For a discussion of the pronunciation of the Middle Atlantic area, see pp. 222-225.
42. Hans Kurath. A Word Geography of the Eastern United States. Ann Arbor: The University of Michigan Press, 1966, pp. 27-28.
43. Albert H. Marckwardt. American English. New York: Oxford University Press, 1958, p. 51.
44. Language in America. New York and Cleveland: The World Publishing Company, 1970, p. 116.
45. Lester W. J. Seifert. "The Word Geography of Pennsylvania German: Extent and Causes," in The German

Language in America. Edited by Glenn G. Gilbert. Austin
and London: University of Texas Press, 1971, p. 19.
     46. Marckwardt, pp. 51-52.
     47. Laird, p. 117.
     48. Applied Phonetics. Englewood Cliffs, N.J.:
Prentice-Hall, Inc., 1957, pp. 403-404.
     49. Ibid., p. 404. For a discussion of the pronun-
ciation of Pennsylvania German, see pages 403-410.

CHAPTER IV: Southern Dialects

     50. Claude Merton Wise. "Speech Regions of Amer-
ica," in Applied Phonetics. Englewood Cliffs, N.J.: Prentice-Hall, Inc., 1957, p. 179.
     51. Cambridge History of American Literature. New
York: Macmillan Company, 1931, II, 365.
     52. "Needed Research in Southern Dialects," in Per-
spectives on the South: Agenda for Research. Edited by Edgar T. Thompson. Durham, N.C.: Duke University Press,
1967, pp. 113-124.
     53. Cultural Regions of the United States. Foreword
by Nathan Glazer. Seattle and London: University of Washington Press, 1975, p. 81.
     54. H. L. Mencken. The American Language. A-
bridged, with annotations and new material by Raven I. Mc-
David, Jr., with the assistance of David W. Maurer. New
York: Alfred A. Knopf, 1971, p. 461.
     55. The Times of Melville and Whitman. New York:
E. P. Dutton, Inc., 1947. Footnote, p. 384.
     56. "Southwestern Vernacular," in Mark Twain: The
Fate of Humor. Princeton, N.J.: Princeton University Press,
1966, p. 167.
     57. Ibid., p. 168.
     58. "Three Problems of Fictional Form: First-Per-
son Narration in David Copperfield and Huckleberry Finn,"
in Experience in the Novel. Edited with a Foreword by Roy
Harvey Pearce. New York: Columbia University Press,
1968, pp. 40-48.
     59. Jay B. Hubbell. Southern Life in Fiction. Ath-
ens: University of Georgia Press, 1960, p. 88.
     60. A Study of Florida Cracker Dialect Based Chiefly
on the Prose Works of Marjorie Kinnan Rawlings. University
of Florida, M.A. Thesis, 1939, p. 9.
     61. "Genesis of the Southern Cracker," American
Mercury, XXV (May, 1935), 106.
     62. McGuire, p. 59.

63. Scribner's, LXXXIX (April, 1931), 366.
64. McGuire, p. 44.

Southern Mountain Dialect

65. Charles Morrow Wilson. "Elizabethan America,"
Atlantic Monthly, CXLIV (July-December, 1929), 238.
66. "Language and Communication Problems in Southern Appalachia," in Contemporary English. Change and Variation. Edited by David L. Shores. Philadelphia: J. B.
Lippincott, 1972, p. 107.
67. "Folk and Folklore," in Culture in the South.
Edited by W. T. Couch. Chapel Hill: University of North
Carolina Press, 1935, pp. 570-571.
68. Maristan Chapman. "American Speech as
Practised in the Southern Highlands," Century, CXVII (March,
1929), 617.
69. Applied Phonetics. New York: Prentice-Hall,
Inc. , 1957, p. 303.
70. "Beefsteak When I'm Hungry," The Virginia
Quarterly Review, VI (April, 1930), 240.
71. "Language of the Southern Highlanders," PMLA,
XLVI (1931), 1302-1322.
72. "Southern Mountain Dialect," American Speech,
XV (February, 1940), 45-54.
73. "The East Tennessee Background of Sidney Lanier's Tiger-Lilies," American Literature, XIX (March, 1947-
January, 1948), 131.
74. Immortal Shadows. New York: Charles Scribner's Sons, 1948, p. 90.
75. Robert Penn Warren, "Elizabeth Madox Roberts:
Life Is from Within," Introduction to The Time of Man. New
York: The Viking Press, 1963. Compass Books Edition,
pp. viii-ix.
76. Ibid. , pp. xiv-xv.
77. "Elizabeth Madox Roberts," in The Spyglass,
Views and Reviews, 1924-1930. Selected and Edited by John
Tyree Fain. Nashville, Tenn. : Vanderbilt University Press,
1963, p. 19.
78. "The Novelist's Use of Dialect," The Writer,
XLVII (January, 1935), 40.
79. "Rhetoric in Southern Writing: Wolfe," The
Georgia Review, XII (Spring, 1958), 82.
80. Letter to Hamilton Basso, July 13, 1937, in The
Letters of Thomas Wolfe. Collected and with an Introduction
and Explanatory Text by Elizabeth Nowell. New York: Charles Scribner's Sons, 1956, p. 625.

81. Herschel Gower, "Introduction," The Hawk's Done Gone and Other Stories. Nashville, Tenn.: Vanderbilt University Press, 1968. Copyright by Mildred Haun, 1940.

82. "Foreword" to Cloud-Walking. New York: Farrar and Rinehart, Inc., 1942, p. v.

Negro Dialect

83. Black English. New York: Random House, 1972, pp. 229, 262.

84. "Observations (1966) on the Problems of Defining Negro Dialect," The Florida FL Reporter, IX, Nos. 1 and 2 (Spring/Fall, 1971), 47-49, 57.

85. "Continuity and Change in American Negro Dialects," in Readings in American Dialectology. Edited by Harold B. Allen and Gary N. Underwood. New York: Appleton-Century-Crofts, 1971, p. 455.

86. Ibid., pp. 466-467.

87. "The Relationship of the Speech of American Negroes to the Speech of Whites," American Speech, XXVI (February, 1951), 3-17.

88. "Biracial Dialectology: Six Years Into the Georgia Survey," Journal of English Linguistics, IX (March, 1975), 21.

89. "Negro Dialect in Eighteenth-Century American Drama," American Speech, XXX (1955), 269-276.

90. Ibid., p. 176.

91. "The Negro in the American Theatre," in American Playwrights on Drama. Edited by Horst Frenz. New York: Hill and Wang, 1965, p. 165.

92. "Introduction," Dark Symphony. Negro Literature in America. Edited by James A. Emanuel and Theodore L. Gross. New York: The Free Press, 1968, p. 3.

93. "Poe's Use of Negro Dialect in 'The Gold Bug,'" in Studies in Languages and Linguistics in Honor of Charles C. Fries. Edited by Albert H. Marckwardt. Ann Arbor, Michigan: English Language Institute, University of Michigan, 1964, p. 269.

94. "Poe's Treatment of the Negro and of the Negro Dialect," University of Texas Studies in English, XVI (July, 1936), 112.

95. Rayburn S. Moore, "Thomas Dunn English, a Forgotten Contributor to the Development of Negro Dialect Verse in the 1870's," American Literature, XXXII (March, 1961-January, 1962), 72-75. See the following poems: "Caesar Rowan," Scribner's Monthly, II (July, 1871), 300;

and "Momma Phoebe," Scribner's Monthly, III (November, 1871), 62-63.

96. "The Negro in American Literature," in The New Negro. Edited by Alain Locke. New York: Johnson Reprint Corporation, 1968, p. 32.

97. "Straight to Heaven," Saturday Review, XXI (December 4, 1948), 20.

98. American Playwrights, 1918-1938. Freeport, N.Y.: Books for Libraries Press, 1966, p. 28.

99. "The Wet Sponge of Eugene O'Neill," in Dialogue in American Drama. Bloomington, Ind.: Indiana University Press, 1971, p. 10.

100. To Make a Poet Black. Chapel Hill: University of North Carolina Press, 1939, pp. 51-52.

101. The Book of American Negro Poetry. New York: Harcourt, Brace and World, Inc., 1922, 1931. Harbrace Paperbound Library, Revised Edition, 1950, 1959, p. 64. Five of Campbell's dialect poems are included.

102. Afro-American Writing, An Anthology of Prose and Poetry. Edited by Richard A. Long and Eugenia W. Collier. New York: New York University Press, 1972, II, 423.

The Gullah Dialect

103. "There is abundant evidence, ... that it or a transitional dialect based on it, is still widely spoken, even in metropolitan Charleston, and even by some whites." Jim Haskins and Hugh F. Butts. The Psychology of Black Language. New York: Barnes and Noble Books, 1973, p. 59.

104. Lorenzo D. Turner. Africanisms in the Gullah Dialect. Chicago: University of Chicago Press, 1949; rpt. Arno Press, 1969, p. 3.

105. M. M. Mathews. Some Sources of Southernisms. University, Alabama: University of Alabama Press, 1948, pp. 92-93.

106. "Gullah: A Negro Patois," The South Atlantic Quarterly, VII (1908), 332-347; VIII (1909), 39-52.

107. Folk Culture on St. Helena Island, South Carolina. Foreword by Don Yoder, 1930; rpt. Hathboro, Pa.: Folklore Associates, Inc., 1968, p. 6.

108. Johnson, p. 3.

109. Bennett, VII, 341.

110. Johnson, pp. 11-12.

111. "Foreword," The Black Border. Gullah Stories of the Carolina Coast. Columbia, S.C.: The State Company, 1922, p. 10.

112. Turner, p. v.
113. Ibid., p. 7.
114. "Gullah," in Ebony and Topaz, a Collectanea.
Edited by Charles S. Johnson, 1927; rpt. Freeport, N.Y.:
Books for Libraries Press, 1971, p. 35.
115. "The Relationship of the Speech of American
Negroes to the Speech of Whites," American Speech, XXVI
(February, 1951), 11-12.
116. Bennett, VII, 337.
117. Bennett, VIII, 52.
118. Johnson, p. 17.
119. Slave Songs of the United States. Edited by W.
F. Allen, Charles Pickard Ware, and Lucy McKim Garrison.
New York: A. Simpson and Company, 1867; rpt. Peter
Smith, 1951, pp. xxiii-xxxvi.
120. "Glossary," in The Old Types Pass. Boston:
The Christopher Publishing House, 1925, pp. 159-165.
121. Gullah. Bulletin of the University of South
Carolina, No. 190, 1926, pp. 24-25.
122. Studies in Area Linguistics. Bloomington:
Indiana University Press, 1972, p. 119.
123. Roll, Jordan, Roll. Indianapolis, Indiana:
Bobbs-Merrill Company, 1933, p. 23.
124. "My Gullah Brother and I: Exploration into a
Community's Language and Myth Through Its Oral Tradition,"
in Black English, A Seminar. Edited by Deborah Sears Harrison and Tom Trabasso. Hillsdale, N.J.: Laurence Erlbaum Associates, Publishers, 1976, pp. 138-144.
125. Gonzales, pp. 12-13.
126. "Poe's Treatment of the Negro and of the Negro Dialect," University of Texas Studies in English, XVI
(1936), 113.
127. "Poe's Use of Negro Dialect in 'The Gold Bug,'"
Studies in Language and Linguistics in Honor of Charles C.
Fries. Edited by Albert H. Marckwardt. Ann Arbor, Michigan: English Language Institute, University of Michigan,
1964, p. 269.
128. J. Allen Morris. "The Stories of William Gilmore Simms," American Literature, XIV (March, 1942), 29.
129. Ibid., p. 30.
130. Ibid., p. 47.
131. Ibid., p. 46, Footnote 3.
132. Ibid., p. 53.
133. Ibid., pp. 48-51.
134. Gullah and Backwoods Dialect in Selected Works
by William Gilmore Simms. Ph.D. dissertation, University
of South Carolina, 1971. Ann Arbor, Mich.: University
Microfilms, 1971, p. 110.

135. Smith, p. 20.
136. Gullah: Negro Life in the Carolina Sea Islands.
Durham, N. C. : Duke University Press, 1940. Ann Arbor:
University Microfilms, 1968, p. 110.
137. "Continuity and Change in American Negro Dialects, " The Florida FL Reporter 6, No. 1 (Spring, 1968),
3-4, 14-16, 18. Rpt. in Readings in American Dialectology.
Edited by Harold B. Allen and Gary N. Underwood. New
York: Appleton-Century-Crofts, 1971, p. 458, Footnote 13.
138. Quoted in Smith, p. 20, Footnote 23.
139. The Spyglass, Views and Reviews, 1924-1930.
Selected and Edited by John Tyree Fain. Nashville, Tenn. :
Vanderbilt University Press, 1963, p. 22.
140. Frank M. Durham. DuBose Heyward, the Man
Who Wrote Porgy. Columbia, S. C. : University of South
Carolina Press, 1954; rpt. Port Washington, N. Y. : Kennikat Press, Inc. , 1965, p. 114.
141. For a discussion of Elliott and his writings,
see Louis D. Rubin, Jr. "William Elliott Shoots a Bear, "
in William Elliott Shoots a Bear. Essays on the Southern
Literary Imagination. Baton Rouge: Louisiana State University Press, 1975, pp. 1-27.
142. Reed Smith, p. 17.
143. "Preface, " Nigger to Nigger. New York:
Charles Scribner's Sons, 1928, pp. vii-viii.
144. Stewart, in Readings in American Dialectology,
p. 466, footnote 26.
145. The Civilization of the Old South. Writings of
Clement Eaton. Edited with an Introduction by Albert D.
Kirwan. Lexington, Ky. : University of Kentucky Press,
1968, p. 77.
146. Gumbo Ya-Ya, a Collection of Louisiana Folk-
Tales. Compiled by WPA, Louisiana Writers' Project, with
Lyle Saxon, State Director, Edward Dreyer, Assistant State
Director, and Robert Tallant, Special Writer. Boston:
Houghton Mifflin Company, 1945, p. 139.
147. Thad St. Martin, "Cajuns, " Yale Review, n. s. ,
XXVI (Summer, 1937), 860.
148. Gumbo Ya-Ya, pp. 182-183.
149. Lewis Herman and Marguerite Shalett Herman.
American Dialects. New York: Theatre Art Books, 1947,
p. 298.
150. St. Martin, p. 859.
151. Arlin Turner. "Introduction, " Creoles and Cajuns by George W. Cable. Gloucester, Mass. : Peter Smith,
1965, pp. 6-7, 15.

152.   The American Novel and Its Tradition.   Garden
City, N. Y.: Doubleday and Company, 1937.   Anchor Books,
p. 175.
153.   Cultural Regions of the United States.   Seattle:
University of Washington Press, 1975, pp. 204-272.

CHAPTER V: Western Dialects

154.   Lewis Herman and Marguerite Shalett Herman.
American Dialects.   New York: Theatre Art Books, 1947,
p. 298.
155.   Language in America.   New York and London:
The World Publishing Company, 1970, p. 158.   See Map 5,
pp. 156-157.
156.   Ibid.
157.   Cambridge History of American Literature.
New York: Macmillan Company, 1931, II, 363.
158.   At Home and Abroad.   Second Series.   Quoted
in Van Wyck Brooks.   The Times of Melville and Whitman.
New York: E. P. Dutton and Company, Inc., 1947.   Footnote, p. 76.
159.   The English Language in America.   New York:
The Century Company, 1925, I, 236-237.
160.   "Edward Eggleston, Linguist," Philological
Quarterly, XXIV (October, 1945), 175.
161.   Reminiscences of James Whitcomb Riley.
Quoted in Van Wyck Brooks.   The Times of Melville and
Whitman.   New York: E. P. Dutton and Company, Inc.,
1947, pp. 384-385, Footnote.
162.   Crumbling Idols.   Edited by Jane Johnson.
Cambridge, Mass.: Harvard University Press, 1960, p. 62.

CHAPTER VI: Dialects Used by Writers
              of English as a Second Language

163.   "Bernard Malamud: The Magic and the Dread,"
in Contemporaries.   Boston: Little, Brown and Company,
1962, p. 204.

APPENDIX

Rural Florida Dialect in "A Plumb Clare Conscience"

by Kathy A. Sorrels*

Rural Florida speech has definite characteristics of vocabulary, pronunciation, and grammatical forms. It is the language of a common, uncomplicated people. Their speech is enriched by a vivid imagination which enables them to describe everyday living in concrete terms. They mispronounce common words, commit grammatical errors, and slur some of their words. But, according to Raven I. McDavid, Jr., "every dialect is in itself a legitimate form of the language, a valid instrument of human communication, and something worthy of serious study." This paper is an analysis of the dialect used by Marjorie Kinnan Rawlings in her story of the Florida Crackers.

One of the distinguishing characteristics of the Florida Cracker dialect is in the pronunciation. Some of the departures from standard speech are the omission of the first syllable ('shining), the final -ow sound changed to -er (fellers), the omission of the last consonant in words ending in -ing (smokin'), the t sound changed to k (recolleck), the final -ed sound changed to t (drinkt, chanct), elision (orter), the addition of an initial syllable (a-tellin'), the changing of the internal vowel sounds (clare), the mispronunciation of common words (ary), and the omission of the f in of before a noun (o' sleep). Of these ten departures from standard speech, the omission of the first or last sound or syllable is the one repeated the most often in this story. Several times an a is added as a prefix to a word (a-goin'). This may be the result of compounding, but it also adds rhythm to the speech.

_____
*This paper was written by Kathy A. Sorrels when she was a first-semester student in Freshman English at the University of Central Arkansas. Now married to Thomas Nauman, she lives in Peoria, Illinois.

177

The second aspect of the dialect is concerned with word choice and expressions. The Florida Cracker puts emphasis to his words by adding "plumb," "shore," or "done" to a statement ("plumb snaked into"), or he adds to the description by redundancy ("raises up"). Figurative expressions drawn from their own experience of country life abound in their speech. The day begins at "crack o'day," proceeds to "'long in the evenin'," and ends at "good-dark." Their countryside is made up of "black-jack," "piney-woods," "palmeeters," "a leaf-brown branch," and a "plumb naked pond." They have "cat sneezes of laughter" and they can be "noble-timid." Someone they don't like is a "cooter," a "catbird," or a "sapsucker." The Georgia boy "lights out for the hard road," running so fast "he jest tossed over" the stumps in his way. Shiner Tim "plays the rabbit" and outwaits Cooter, who is a "prime bloodhound." Meanwhile the mosquitoes get so thick they are "fightin' for standin' room" and a moccasin comes so close that Tim "could o' spit on him."

Shiner Tim not only switches standard words around to fit his needs, but he also invents words. He feels "froggy" or nervous about his still which hasn't enough "watchment" or guarding. While hiding in the palmettos, he becomes "fondlike" of a root for a pillow and feels "faintified" when a rattlesnake slithers by.

Idiomatic expressions are also used by the Florida Crackers. Someone frightened is "scairt as chickens" and it's "a pore set o' heels cain't save a scairt body." Since the soil is rich and dark, the mud is "black as a nigger's gizzard." And the only show of religion is in Shiner Tim's favorite phrase, "I orter allus let my conscience be my guide."

Another aspect of this dialect is the variations from standard grammatical forms. A common example is that of forming the past tense by adding s to the first person present tense (takes for took). Many times the past tense of strong verbs is formed by analogy with weak verbs (outrunned for outran). Six examples of double negatives are used in the story ("hit ain't no human") and one incorrect form of the superlative ("carelessest"). Another frequent use is the substitution of the auxiliary verbs "have" and "would" with "of" or "done" ("orter done been"). They use "hisself" for "himself," "takes me" for "took myself," and "them scoundrels" for "those scoundrels." Sometimes they run words to-

gether and at other times they add unnecessary words.   This
is usually for emphasis ("jest only Cooter").

Shiner Tim frequently repeats the words "reckon,"
"dogged, " and "like" in his speech.   Other characters use
"reckon" also.   "I reckon not, " says Cooter.   "I reckon for
about thirty days ... " (Shiner Tim); "Reckon they'll be ... "
(Georgia boy); "serves them dogged right" (Shiner Tim).   To
Shiner Tim a squirrel comes down "sudden-like"; the agent
runs in "from the side, like"; "their leaving is a trap, like";
and he hides in the edge of "jest out of the swamp, like. "

Verbs do not always agree with their subjects ("we
was, you was, they comes").   An extra es is added to the
already plural forms ("snakeses" and "antses").   Several
similes are used to describe Shiner Tim: "like a bird dog, "
"like a puffy scarlet Chinaman, " and "like dogged cur'ous
deer. "   His moonshine is "as sound as the best Kentucky
Bourbon. "

A Webster's unabridged dictionary gives this definition
of a Cracker: "An impoverished white person in the rural
sections of the southern United States, especially in Georgia
and Florida. "   The dialect of the Crackers is explained by
this statement.   Having little or no education, being poor
(Tim is a moonshiner), living in a rural region (Florida
swamps), they have developed their dialect naturally.   Drawing on the countryside and country life, they invent new words
or change old ones.   Living in the South, they have the Southern trait of omitting the first or last syllable of a word, of
slurring words, and of drawing others out ("tomorrer").
Their life is not easy so they enjoy recounting a story or
experience to their friends.   Although they misuse the English language, their dialect is not ineffective; "its prestige
comes from the prestige of those who use it. "   Shiner Tim
is worthy of prestige because he is an honest man.   He
makes pure corn liquor and does not use any of the tricks
of the trade as do some of the other moonshiners (cut the
mash with lye).   It took patience and stamina for him to remain hidden in the swamp overnight.   He has many friends
who are worried about his safe return.   And when he finally
returns home, he tells his experience to them in his colorful rural Florida speech.   In standard English his story would
have been flat and thin ("like").

LISTING OF DIALECT MATERIAL IN STORY
FOR USE IN WRITING PAPER

I. Pronunciation

A. Omission of first syllable

'shining	'twa'n't
'shiner's	'em
'til	'bout
'long	

B. Final t sound changed to k

recolleck

C. Final ed sound changed to t

clost	kilt
drinkt	chanct
scairt	

D. Initial syllable substitution

afore for before

E. Final ow sound changed to er

palmeeters	fellers
foller	to-morrer

F. Rev sound changed to iv

chivolay

G. Omission of last sound or syllable

smokin'	evenin'	picklin'
liftin'	lookin'	smashin'
waitin'	talkin'	jes'
standin'-room	quare-lookin'	hittin'
tol'	th'	traipsin'
slappin'	mornin'	crowdin'
sitten'	spendin'	fightin'
goin'	runnin'	'twa'n't
makin'	fixin'	ol'

H. Omission of internal vowel

>   fr'm
>   cur'ous

I. Elision

Hit'll (it will)	'twa'n't (it was not)
t'other (the other)	orter (ought to)
allus (always)	nary (not any)
iffen (if then)	

J. Adding an initial syllable or letter

a-tellin'	a-stingin'	that-a-way
a-cussin'	a-freezin'	hit's (it's)
a-slappin'	a-goin'	a-burnin'
a-smokin'		

K. Changed internal vowel sound

quare	clare	heerd
fur	leetle	mought
oneasy	kin	thu
scairt	palmeeters	git
fust		

L. Mispronunciation of common words

ary	skeeter (short-	pertickler
figgers	ened form of	
yestiddy	mosquitoes)	

M. Omitting f in of before a noun

o'sleep	o'day	o'froggy
o'them	o'spit	o'heels
o'the	o'water	o'blood
o'faintified	o'quare-lookin'	o'gone
o'waitin'	o'me	

II. Words and Expressions

A. Redundancy

raises up	kilt dead	long gone
good gone	a whiles yet	mighty sorry

| buried up | a-burnin' up | swole up |
| smash up | great whiles | heap longer |

B. Plumb, shore, and done used for emphasis or as
    intensifiers

done been	plumb clare
plumb naked pond	shore remember
shore orter	done set
shore chunk	plumb set in
shore kin	done outwaited
shore surrounded	done tol'
plumb snaked	shore a soft pillow

C. Figurative expressions

piney-woods	lowbush corn liquor
pop-eyes	good-dark
mucky of water	'long in the even'
hitched closer	piece o' sleep
plumb naked pond	ground-hog still
quare-lookin' sap-sucker	
dogged cur'our deed	noble-timid boy
plays the rabbit	hemmed in
moved my jawbones	a prime bloodhound
a piece longer	fightin' for standin' room
pure running branch water	
leaf-brown branch	raises up a fuss
crack o' day	cat sneezes of laughter
pottered around	crowdin' on
hog-style	tossed over 'em
could o' spit on him	

D. Original words

| watchment | sudden-like | froggy |
| faintified | fondlike | |

E. Idiomatic expressions

"a pore set o'heels caint save a scairt body"
"scairt as chickens"
"conscience be my guide"

III. Grammatical forms

    A. Past tense formed by adding an <u>s</u> to the present tense form

        begins (began)   takes (took)
        pokes (poked)   sits (sat)
        settles (settled)   jumps (jumped)
        sets (set)   feels (felt)
        looks (looked)   notices (noticed)
        plays (played)   brings (brought)
        beats (beat)   tracks (tracked)
        thinks (thought)   studies (studied)
        goes (went)   stops (stopped)
        gits (got)   says (said)
        crawls (crawled)

    B. Wrong form and pronunciation of past tense

        runned (ran)   drinkt (drank)
        cain't (can not)   outrunned (outran)
        scairt (scared)   seed (saw)
        heerd (heard)   done (did)
        knowed (knew)

    C. Double negative

        hit ain't no human   ain't nary
        'twa'n't no place   not o' gone no
        'twa'n't no use
        ain't goin' to turn into no still

    D. Omission of or substitution for the auxiliary verbs <u>have</u> and <u>would</u>

        they'd of seed me (they would have seen me)
        should of give (should have given)
        orter done been (ought to have been)
        I'd done been (I would have been)
        not o' gone (not have gone)
        I could o' spit (I could have spit)

    E. Wrong form of superlatives

        carelessest (most careless)

F.   Wrong form of pronoun

hisself (himself)   takes me (took myself)
had me (had myself)   them scoundrels (those
                              scoundrels)

G.   Omission of if

see kin I (see if I can)

H.   Addition of unnecessary words

to put me a thing (me)
to git us a piece (us)
jest only Cooter (jest)
scoundrel does squat there (does)
I' orter have (orter)
I've done turkey-hunted (done)
you or me, one (one)

I.   Frequent use of the word like

or mixed-like   from the side, like
a trap, like   out of the swamp, like
fondlike   sudden-like

J.   Wrong form of plurals

snakeses   antses
mosquitoes was (were)   there's times (are)
we was (were)   they was (were)
they makes (make)   they's so (are)
they comes (come)

K.   Substitution of they for there

If they is

L.   Use of similes

Like a bird dog
as sound as the best Kentucky Bourbon
like a puffy scarlet Chinaman
like dogged cur'ous deer
scairt as chickens

INDEX

185

Wright, Nathalie: The East Tennessee Background of Lanier's Tiger-Lilies 26
Wright, Richard 110; Eight Men 111; Native Son 111; Uncle Tom's Children 110

The Yearling (Marjorie Kinnan Rawlings) 60
The Yemassee (William G. Simms) 129
Yiddish and American English (Lillian Mermin Feinsilver) 160
Yiddish Idioms in American English (Lillian Mermin Feinsilver) 160
Yiddish in American Fiction (Alter Brody) 160
Yoked with a Lamb (Helen R. Martin) 43
You Know Me, Al (Ring Lardner) 156